T0159324

FRESH VEGETABLES

Rose Grant

BRISTOL PUBLISHING ENTERPRISES
San Leandro, California

a nitty gritty® cookbook

Printed in the United States of America.

ISBN 1-55867-175-7

Cover design: Frank J. Paredes
Cover photography: John A. Benson
Food styling: Susan Massey
Illustrations: Shanti Nelson
Index: Rose Grant

CONTENTS

To Elena and Alex —
who could have imagined that these small people
could add so much joy to our family!

To the fearless five —
Aaron, Jefferson, Michael, Nile and Reed,
led by Daniel, king of the cousins.
And their parents, who nourish and cherish them.

And, of course, to Philip —
who, after 50 years has not tired of my cooking.
It must be love!

EAT MORE FRESH VEGETABLES

Eat more fresh vegetables and you will (pick one or two): look younger; resist disease; lose weight; have better hair; have more vitality. Claims for health-giving properties of vegetables abound; by now, everyone knows the statistics.

As the variety of vegetables available year-round increases, so do the number of vegetable cookbooks. In *Fresh Vegetables*, ease of purchase and ease of preparation are stressed. All vegetables in this book can be found in most supermarkets, and most recipes take no more than 25 minutes to prepare.

I am often amused by the admonition: Use only the freshest, highest quality produce. It's great advice, but who can follow it? True, fresh vegetables should be harvested and purchased as close to eating time as possible; aging them in the refrigerator does not enhance their taste, nor their nutritive value. However, not many of us have access to just-picked vegetables, nor is a daily trip to the market part of most people's schedule.

Often, skillful preparation and the addition of herbs and spices can rescue a zucchini that is beginning to soften or potatoes that have started to sprout. Think of what you can do with an ordinary carrot! You can serve it in the style of Morocco, in a spicy soup, as a main dish with bulgur, or with white wine for a company dinner; and the recipes are all in *Fresh Vegetables*.

Ethnic cooks know well how to use the harvest. Vegetables, combined with rice, form the backbone of Chinese dishes. With pasta, vegetables are an integral part of Italian meals. Middle-eastern cuisines mix vegetables with bulgur to make delicious pilafs. Meat, if used, is often a garnish in ethnic recipes.

Steaming is the simplest way to cook vegetables, but they can also be broiled, roasted or grilled. Many cooks will spend hours to create an elaborate main dish or dessert, but vegetables have just a few minutes to prove themselves before their time runs out. Vegetable preparation can't be a big deal. Fortunately, most vegetables are very accommodating and actually benefit from little handling.

A word about the recipes: The recipes in this book are organized according to the time of year that they normally grow. However, many types of vegetables are now available all year. I am rather casual about amounts; taste is what counts and it's fine to alter proportions to suit your own palate. Very few of my recipes contain large amounts of lip-searing spices; I do not think that eating should be painful. But many people love hot foods. These recipes lend themselves to your individual interpretation. With your own modifications, my recipe becomes your signature dish and it doesn't matter at all that it bears no resemblance to the original. If you think about it, isn't that how most new recipes are born?

VEGETABLE DISHES FOR SPRING AND SUMMER

ROASTED ARTICHOKES

In a way, roasted artichokes are easier to prepare than steamed artichokes. Once they're in the oven, you can go on to other things. Roasting seems to bring out the natural sweetness of the artichokes. They can be served with a garlic mayonnaise or just plain with a squirt of lemon.

4 large artichokes
juice of 1 large lemon
2-3 tbs. olive oil
2 cloves garlic, finely chopped

salt and pepper to taste
several sprigs fresh thyme or sage
$\frac{1}{4}$ cup dry white wine or water

Heat oven to 400°. Snap off tough outer leaves of artichokes and slice off the thorny tops. Cut artichokes into quarters, or sixths if very large, and remove fuzzy chokes with a spoon. Drop prepared artichokes into a bowl of water with lemon juice to prevent them from turning brown. Lightly coat a glass or ceramic baking dish (do not use metal) with 2 to 3 tbs. olive oil. Remove artichokes from water and drain well. Place artichokes in a single layer in pan. Sprinkle with garlic, salt, pepper, thyme and white wine. Cover with waxed paper and cover waxed paper with aluminum foil; foil should not touch artichokes. Place in oven and roast for about 30 minutes. Remove cover and roast for 20 to 25 minutes, stirring occasionally, until artichokes are tender and just beginning to brown; they should be slightly crisp. Serve hot or cold.

PASTA WITH ARUGULA AND SWEET ONIONS

Servings: 6-8

This is a perfect summer dish. Hot pasta and cold sauce is just right for lunch or supper. The sauce should not be cooked. Tri-colored fusilli makes a lovely presentation. Sweet onions are mild, juicy young onions that are available during the spring and early summer months. The best-known varieties are Walla Walla, from Washington state; Vidalia, from Georgia; and Maui, from Hawaii.

2 cups coarsely chopped sweet onions
2 lb. small ripe tomatoes, quartered
2 cloves garlic, minced
1 tbs. small capers
1/2 cup olive oil
2 tbs. wine vinegar

salt and pepper to taste
1 lb. fusilli pasta
1/2 bunch fresh basil, leaves only
1 lb. arugula, coarse stems removed
2 tbs. grated Parmesan cheese, optional

In a medium bowl, combine onions, tomatoes, garlic, capers, oil, vinegar, salt and pepper; mix well and refrigerate. Cook pasta in a large pot of boiling salted water until slightly firm to the bite, *al dente*; drain.

Thoroughly wash and dry basil and arugula and arrange on a large platter. Place hot pasta on top. Pour cold sauce over pasta and serve with grated cheese, if desired.

ASPARAGUS AND RICE GRATIN

This is a great side dish for a spring meal. It can also be a vegetarian entrée. Thin or medium-thick asparagus stalks work best; discard the tough ends. Instead of boiling, you can cook the asparagus in a microwave on HIGH for about 5 minutes; it should be underdone.

2 lb. asparagus, cut into 1½-inch pieces
1 cup long-grain rice
2 cups chicken stock
3 eggs, beaten until frothy
1 cup milk

½ cup half-and-half
salt and pepper to taste
½ tsp. nutmeg
¼ cup grated Parmesan cheese

Cook asparagus in boiling water until slightly underdone, no more than 8 minutes; drain. Separate asparagus tips from stalks. Cut stalks into 2-inch pieces. In a saucepan, combine rice with chicken stock and bring to a full boil. Cover and immediately reduce heat to low. Simmer for about 15 minutes. Combine asparagus stalks, rice, eggs, milk, half-and-half, salt, pepper and nutmeg. Transfer to a baking dish and bake for about 20 minutes, until eggs are set. Top with asparagus tips, sprinkle with Parmesan and bake for another 5 minutes. Serve hot.

ASPARAGUS AND
SUN-DRIED TOMATO SALAD

This visually appealing salad has an interesting combination of flavors and is a lovely complement to a spring meal.

1 lb. fresh thin asparagus spears, tough ends trimmed
6 cups mixed baby salad greens or torn red leaf lettuce
1/2 cup chopped purple onion, or more to taste
6 large oil-packed sun-dried tomatoes, drained, chopped
1/3 cup olive oil
1-2 tbs. balsamic vinegar
1 tbs. Dijon mustard, or less to taste
salt and pepper to taste
3 tbs. chopped fresh dill, or less to taste
1 tsp. dried mixed Italian herbs
1 cup shredded fontina cheese

Cut asparagus into 2-inch lengths. Cook or steam asparagus until tender-crisp, about 5 to 6 minutes. Drain asparagus, rinse with cold water and pat dry. In a large bowl, combine asparagus with greens, onion and tomatoes. In a small jar, combine olive oil with vinegar, mustard, salt, pepper and herbs. Cover and shake well. At serving time, add cheese to salad and toss with salad dressing.

CURRIED ASPARAGUS SOUP

Servings: 8

Here's a special soup to welcome spring. You can use most of the asparagus for the soup, but save the tips for garnishing.

2 lb. asparagus, tough ends trimmed
1/4 cup butter
2 large leeks, washed thoroughly, chopped
1 large potato, peeled, sliced
1 can (46 oz.) chicken broth
1-2 cups dry white wine
salt and pepper to taste
1 tbs. chopped fresh tarragon, or 1 tsp. dried
2 tbs. curry powder
1 pt. half-and-half
chopped fresh dill for garnish

Cook asparagus in boiling water until tips are tender-crisp, about 5 minutes. Remove asparagus tips and reserve. Cut asparagus stalks into 2-inch pieces. Melt butter in a large saucepan over medium heat. Sauté asparagus stalks, leeks and potato for about 5 minutes. Add broth, wine, salt, pepper, tarragon and curry powder. Cover and cook until vegetables are very tender, about 15 to 20 minutes. Cool. Puree mixture with a blender or food processor and return to saucepan. Add half-and-half and asparagus tips and simmer over low heat for 5 minutes; the soup should not boil. Garnish with dill and serve.

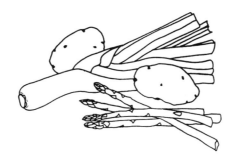

GAZPACHO

There must be a million recipes for gazpacho, but give this a try. It's simple to prepare with a slightly different taste from the Clamato juice. The spiciness and vegetable proportions can be varied to suit your taste.

1 jar (46 oz.) Clamato juice
1 can (46 oz.) V-8 juice
3 cups mixed chopped celery, cucumber, garlic, flat-leaf parsley,
    red and green bell peppers and green onions
1/3 cup red wine vinegar
1/3 cup lemon juice
3 tbs. olive oil
1/2 tsp. hot pepper sauce, or more to taste
1/2 tsp. chili powder, or less to taste
salt and pepper to taste
1 can (16 oz.) stewed tomatoes with juice

In a large bowl, combine juices. Finely chop vegetables by hand or with a food processor and add to bowl with juice. Combine vinegar, lemon juice, oil, pepper sauce, chili powder, salt and pepper and add to juice-vegetable mixture. Add stewed tomatoes and mix well. Refrigerate until very cold to blend flavors.

GREEN PEA SOUP WITH MINT

This is a simple soup that can also be made any time with frozen peas. It takes very little time to prepare. It is particularly good icy cold, but it can be served hot as well.

2 tbs. butter
1 large onion, chopped
1 large potato, coarsely chopped
2 lb. fresh shelled peas, or 1 pkg.
    (20 oz.) frozen peas
1 can (46 oz.) chicken broth

1 tbs. sugar
2-3 tbs. chopped fresh mint, or
    2 tsp. dried
salt and pepper to taste
1 cup light cream or half-and-half
chopped fresh mint for garnish

Melt butter in a large saucepan over medium-high heat. Sauté onion and potato for about 5 minutes. Add peas, chicken broth, sugar, 2 to 3 tbs. mint, salt and pepper and simmer for about 20 minutes. Puree mixture with a food processor or blender until smooth. Return mixture to pan, add cream and stir to blend. For hot soup, heat gently just until heated through; do not boil. For cold soup, chill thoroughly. When ready to serve, garnish with chopped fresh mint.

FAVA BEANS, GREEN PEAS, ARTICHOKES AND RICOTTA

Servings: 6-8

This is a spring or summer dish that takes practically no time to prepare. Serve it over fettuccine or spaghetti for a complete meal.

1½ lb. fresh fava beans, shelled, tough outer skins removed,
   or 2 pkg. (10 oz. each) frozen fava beans, thawed,
   or 2 cans (15 oz. each) fava beans, drained
1½ lb. fresh shelled green peas, or 2 pkg.
   (10 oz. each) frozen peas, thawed
1 lb. fettuccine or spaghetti
2 tbs. butter
2 tbs. olive oil
3 shallots, finely chopped
2 jars (6 oz.) marinated artichokes, drained
2 tbs. lemon juice
2 tbs. finely chopped fresh flat-leaf parsley
2 tbs. shredded fresh basil leaves, or more to taste
salt and pepper to taste
½ lb. fresh ricotta cheese, room temperature
grated Parmesan cheese

In a large pan of boiling water, cook fava beans and fresh peas until just tender, about 8 to 10 minutes; drain. Do not cook frozen peas. In a large pot of boiling salted water, cook pasta until slightly firm to the bite, *al dente*. While pasta is cooking, heat butter and olive oil in a medium skillet over medium heat. Add shallots and sauté until limp. Add cooked beans, peas and artichokes and sauté until heated through. Place cooked pasta in a large bowl and toss with vegetables, lemon juice, parsley, basil, salt and pepper. With your fingers, separate ricotta into small clumps and add to pasta mixture. Serve hot. Pass Parmesan cheese.

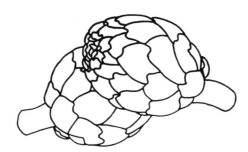

GINGER PEAS WITH WATER CHESTNUTS

This is an interesting combination that goes with meat or chicken. The water chestnuts give this dish an appealing crunch.

2 tbs. butter
½ lb. domestic or wild mushrooms,
   sliced
1 clove garlic, minced
¼ cup sliced water chestnuts, patted dry
½ cup green onion pieces, 1-inch pieces
1 tsp. grated fresh ginger, or more
   to taste

salt and pepper to taste
½ tsp. nutmeg
2 lb. fresh shelled green peas, or 2 pkg.
   (10 oz. each) frozen peas, thawed
1 cup chicken stock
2 tbs. cornstarch
2 tbs. water

Melt butter in a large skillet over medium-high heat. Add mushrooms, garlic, water chestnuts and green onions and sauté for 3 minutes. Add ginger, salt, pepper, nutmeg, peas and chicken stock and cook for 5 minutes or less, just until peas soften. Combine cornstarch with water, add to mixture and stir until thick. Serve immediately.

SNOW PEAS AND MUSHROOMS WITH ALMONDS

Crunchy snow peas are a welcome change from the usual vegetables. If the peas seem limp, soak them in ice water for 30 minutes or longer. Use any kind of mushrooms or combine white mushrooms with shiitakes or portobellos.

2 tbs. butter
1 clove garlic, minced
½ cup sliced green onions, with some
   of the green tops
1½ lb. fresh snow peas, strings
   removed
½ lb. mushrooms, sliced
2 tbs. cornstarch

1 cup water
1 chicken bouillon cube, or 1 tsp.
   chicken bouillon granules
salt and pepper to taste
1 tbs. soy sauce
3 tbs. sliced almonds, toasted
chopped fresh cilantro for garnish

In a large skillet, melt butter over medium heat. Sauté garlic and green onions for 3 minutes. Add snow peas and mushrooms and sauté for 3 to 5 minutes, until snow peas are tender-crisp. Combine cornstarch and water and stir until smooth. Add to skillet with bouillon, salt, pepper and soy sauce; stir until hot and thick. Top with sliced almonds and chopped cilantro. Serve immediately.

SUGAR SNAP PEAS WITH MUSHROOMS

Servings: 6

Try this in the summer when sugar snap peas are at their very best. The peas are usually so tender that they can be eaten raw. It is important not to overcook them.

1 tbs. vegetable oil
1 tbs. butter
2 cloves garlic, finely minced
1 lb. sugar snap peas
½ lb. portobello or other mushrooms, sliced
1 tbs. soy sauce
2 tbs. sesame seeds, toasted

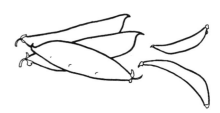

In a large skillet or wok, heat oil and butter over medium-high heat until bubbly. Add minced garlic and stir-fry for 1 minute. Add sugar snap peas and mushrooms and stir-fry for 3 to 4 minutes, until peas are just tender-crisp. Stir in soy sauce to coat peas and mushrooms. Sprinkle with sesame seeds and serve.

SUGAR SNAP PEAS WITH PROSCIUTTO AND MINT

Peas with crunch add a special feeling to an ordinary side dish. Sugar snaps used to be available just in the summer, but now you can get them throughout the year.

1½ lb. sugar snap peas
1 tbs. olive oil
2-3 shallots, chopped
2-3 oz. prosciutto, imported preferred, fat trimmed, chopped
salt and pepper to taste
2 tbs. chopped fresh mint

Steam sugar snap peas for 3 to 4 minutes until just tender-crisp; do not overcook. Just before serving, heat olive oil in a skillet over medium heat. Add shallots and sauté until limp. Add sugar snap peas, prosciutto, salt and pepper and sauté for 2 minutes. Top with fresh mint and serve.

BULGUR SALAD

This salad can be a vegetarian meal or a lovely first course. Add bread with slices of feta cheese for a substantial lunch. Look for bulgur (processed cracked wheat) in the supermarket near the rice or in the bulk bins.

2 cups water
1 cup bulgur wheat
3 tbs. lemon juice, or more to taste
1/4 cup olive oil
salt and pepper to taste
1 small cucumber, peeled, cut into cubes
2 medium-sized ripe tomatoes, cut into chunks, or 2 cups cherry tomatoes
1 red or green bell pepper, cut into strips
1 bunch green onions, with some of the green tops, chopped
1/4 cup finely chopped fresh flat-leaf parsley
2 tbs. finely chopped fresh mint
sliced black olives to taste, optional

In a 2-quart saucepan, bring water to a boil. Add bulgur in a slow stream so that water continues to boil. Stir bulgur, cover pan, immediately reduce heat to low and simmer for about 10 minutes, until all water has been absorbed. Remove cover and cook for 1 to 2 minutes, stirring frequently, to dry the grains. Transfer bulgur to a large bowl. Mix together lemon juice and olive oil and add to bulgur while still warm. Cool mixture to room temperature and season with salt and pepper. Stir in cucumber, tomatoes, bell pepper and green onions and chill until serving time. Just before serving, add parsley, mint and olives, if using.

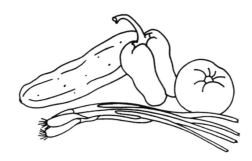

CORN AND MUSHROOM RAGOUT

Servings: 6

This simple dish can be prepared ahead of time and reheated. Frozen corn can be substituted for fresh corn, but the dish loses something. Do not substitute dried sage, as the flavor will not be the same.

3 tbs. olive or safflower oil
1 red onion, thinly sliced
4 cloves garlic, finely chopped, or to taste
1 large yellow bell pepper, cut into 1-inch strips
1/2 lb. mushrooms, such as portobello, shiitake and/or white
6 Roma tomatoes, coarsely chopped
salt and pepper to taste
4 cups fresh corn kernels, from about 6 ears corn
6 fresh sage leaves, finely chopped
chopped fresh flat-leaf parsley for garnish

Heat oil over medium heat in a large skillet. Add onion and garlic and sauté until limp, about 2 to 3 minutes. Add pepper, mushrooms, tomatoes, salt and pepper and sauté for 3 to 4 minutes. Add corn kernels and sage and cook for about 5 minutes, stirring occasionally. Serve topped with chopped parsley.

CORN, GREEN PEA
AND MUSHROOM MEDLEY

This quick-to-fix recipe is a wonderful summer mix. The proportions are not important, but try to get some of each vegetable for the color variety. Remove corn kernels from the cob by slicing down with a sharp knife. Fresh garden tomatoes make this dish even more special.

½ lb. or more shelled fresh green peas, or 1 pkg. (10 oz.) frozen petite peas, thawed
1 tbs. butter
1 tbs. corn oil
2 large shallots, chopped (about ¼ cup)
½ lb. fresh white or wild mushrooms, sliced

3 cups fresh corn, from about 4 ears corn
½ tsp. sugar
salt and pepper to taste
2 tbs. chopped fresh dill
2 garden tomatoes, cut into wedges, optional

If using fresh peas, cook in boiling water until barely tender, about 8 to 10 minutes; drain. Heat butter and oil in a large saucepan. Add shallots and sauté for about 1 minute. Add mushrooms and sauté for about 1 minute. Add corn, peas, sugar, salt and pepper and cook until corn and peas are very tender, about 3 to 5 minutes. Top with fresh dill and tomatoes, if using, and serve immediately.

TEX-MEX CORN AND SWEET POTATO SOUP

Servings: 6-8

This soup contains no fat. It can be "hottened up" or "cooled down," depending on individual taste. Jalapeño or Anaheim chiles will provide mild to moderate heat; habanero chiles can bring tears to your eyes.

1 large onion, chopped
2 large cloves garlic, minced
1-2 small chiles, seeded and chopped
salt and pepper to taste
2 tsp. ground cumin, or more to taste
4 cups vegetable stock or water
juice of 2 limes

1 large sweet potato, coarsely chopped
1 small red bell pepper, chopped
3 cups fresh corn kernels, from about
    4 ears corn, or 1 pkg. (20 oz.)
    frozen corn
finely chopped fresh cilantro for garnish
lime wedges for garnish

In a large saucepan, combine all ingredients, except corn and garnishes. Cover and simmer for about 20 minutes, until sweet potato is soft. Add 1/2 of the corn and cook for 5 minutes. Puree soup with a food processor or blender until smooth and return to saucepan. Add remaining corn and cook until kernels are tender, about 5 minutes. Sprinkle with cilantro and serve with lime wedges.

CORN PUDDING

This is a great dish to prepare in the summer when there is an abundance of fresh corn, but it is also good with frozen corn or even canned corn (in a pinch). Bake the pudding in a quiche dish; it makes a lovely presentation.

3 eggs
1/4 cup flour
2 tbs. sugar
1 tsp. baking powder
salt and pepper to taste
1 cup half-and-half
2 cups fresh corn kernels, from about
   3 ears fresh corn

1/4 cup butter, melted
3 green onions, finely chopped
2 tbs. chopped fresh flat-leaf parsley
2 tbs. chopped fresh chives
2 tbs. chopped fresh dill
3/4 cup grated cheddar cheese

Heat oven to 350°. In a bowl, beat eggs until blended. Add flour, sugar, baking powder, salt, pepper and half-and-half. Mix well. Stir in corn and remaining ingredients and pour into a buttered baking dish. Bake for about 40 minutes, until eggs are set.

ITALIAN-STYLE EGGPLANT

Servings: 6-8

This makes a hearty appetizer with bread or crackers or a satisfying sandwich filling for pita bread. The eggplant can also be cooked in a microwave if you are pressed for time: pierce the eggplant with a fork, place it on paper towels and cook on HIGH for about 20 minutes.

2 large eggplants
2 tbs. olive or vegetable oil
1 large onion, chopped
3-4 cloves garlic, chopped
1 green bell pepper, chopped
1 red bell pepper, chopped
3 stalks celery, chopped, optional
1 can (8 oz.) tomato sauce
1 can (6 oz.) tomato paste
1 cup water, or more if needed
2 tbs. brown sugar
salt and pepper to taste
2 tsp. paprika
2 tsp. mixed dried Italian herbs

Heat oven to 350°. Prick eggplants with a fork in several places. Place eggplants on a baking sheet and bake for about 1 hour, or until very tender. Cool and remove skin. Coarsely mash eggplant flesh. Heat oil in a large skillet. Add onion, garlic, peppers and celery, if using, and sauté for about 10 minutes, until vegetables are tender. Add mashed eggplant and cook for a few more minutes. Add remaining ingredients and simmer uncovered for about 2 hours, stirring often. Add more water if mixture seems too dry; mixture should be thick. Serve cold or at room temperature.

PASTA WITH TANGY ASIAN EGGPLANT

The natural sweetness of the slender violet Asian eggplant combines beautifully with the pasta and the other ingredients to make a satisfying main dish. Pour boiling water over the tomatoes to make them peel easily. Small pieces of canned or fresh tuna fish can be added for an additional flavor.

1 lb. medium shell pasta
6 tbs. olive oil
3 cloves garlic, finely chopped
2 long, slender Asian eggplants, peeled or unpeeled, cut into 1/2-inch cubes
1 small green bell pepper, cut into 1/2-inch pieces
1 small red bell pepper, cut into 1/2-inch pieces
6-8 Roma tomatoes, peeled, coarsely chopped
2 tbs. raisins, golden preferred

2 tbs. drained capers
1 tbs. sugar, or less to taste
2 tbs. balsamic or red wine vinegar
2 tbs. finely chopped fresh flat-leaf parsley
2 tbs. chopped fresh basil
1 tbs. chopped fresh oregano, or 1 tsp. dried
salt and pepper to taste
2 cans (6 1/2 oz. each) tuna fish, drained, flaked, optional

Cook pasta in a large amount of boiling salted water until slightly firm to the bite, *al dente;* drain immediately. While pasta is cooking, heat olive oil over medium-high heat in a large skillet. Add garlic and sauté until garlic begins to sizzle. Add eggplant and peppers and sauté for about 2 to 3 minutes, until vegetables begin to soften. Add remaining ingredients, except tuna, and cook for 5 minutes. Add tuna, if using, and cook until heated through. Combine mixture with hot pasta, toss to coat evenly and serve immediately.

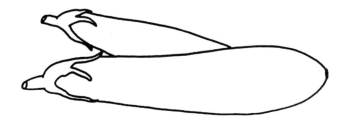

SWEET-AND-SOUR EGGPLANT

Servings: 6-8

Serve this dish to people who say they don't like eggplant; it's a mind-changer. It combines wonderfully with Middle Eastern dishes or roasted meats, and it is an unusual antipasto offering.

2 lb. eggplant, unpeeled, cut lengthwise
    into ¼-inch-thick slices
olive oil
salt and pepper to taste
½ cup red wine vinegar
3 tbs. olive oil

1 tbs. honey
1 tsp. sugar
1 tbs. chopped fresh flat-leaf parsley
1 tbs. chopped fresh basil
1 tbs. chopped fresh mint

Heat broiler. Place eggplant on a nonaluminum baking sheet (stainless steel is fine). Brush with olive oil and broil until eggplant is soft and lightly browned. Turn and broil the other side. Remove slices as they brown and keep warm; do not let eggplant burn. Season eggplant with salt and pepper. In a bowl, combine remaining ingredients. Place warm eggplant in a locking plastic bag or dish and add marinade. Seal bag or cover bowl and marinate eggplant for at least 1 hour and up to 1 day. Discard marinade. Serve at room temperature. Eggplant can be stored in the refrigerator for up to 3 days.

CARAWAY GREEN BEANS

Enliven an everyday vegetable with just a few additions.

1 lb. green beans, ends trimmed, cut into 2-inch pieces
2 tbs. butter
2 tbs. chopped onion
1 clove garlic, finely minced
1 tbs. flour
1/2 cup sour cream or plain yogurt
1/2 cup milk
1/2 tsp. sugar
salt and pepper to taste
1/2 cup coarsely grated cheddar cheese, or more to taste
1/2 tsp. caraway seeds

Steam green beans until tender-crisp, about 5 minutes; drain and keep warm. Melt butter in a skillet over medium heat. Add onion and garlic and sauté until wilted. Add flour and stir until combined. Combine remaining ingredients and add to skillet. Cook, stirring, until cheese is melted; do not boil. Pour cheese mixture over hot drained green beans and mix gently. Serve immediately.

GREEN BEANS WITH CHÈVRE

This simple green bean dish becomes company fare with the addition of chèvre (soft white goat cheese).

1½ lb. young green beans, ends trimmed,
    cut into 2-inch pieces
3-4 tbs. crumbled chèvre
1-2 tbs. chopped fresh dill
2 green onions, chopped
2 tbs. lemon juice
salt and pepper to taste

Steam green beans until tender-crisp, about 5 minutes; drain and keep warm. Combine remaining ingredients and pour over warm beans. Toss until coated. Serve immediately.

GREEN BEANS WITH HAZELNUTS

Hazelnuts and shallots added to green beans put this dish in the "special" category. There's really nothing to it.

½ cup finely chopped lightly toasted hazelnuts
⅓ cup dry breadcrumbs
1½ lb. green beans, ends trimmed, cut into 2-inch pieces
6 tbs. butter
2-3 tbs. minced shallots
salt and pepper to taste
chopped fresh dill to taste

Combine nuts and breadcrumbs and set aside. Partially cook green beans in boiling salted water for about 3 minutes; drain. Heat butter in a large skillet over medium heat. Add shallots and sauté until softened. Add green beans and breadcrumb mixture. Sauté for several minutes to heat through. Add salt, pepper and chopped dill. Serve at once.

GREEN BEANS WITH TOMATOES AND GARLIC

This is a great summer standby when beans and tomatoes are at their peak. It works almost as well with drained canned tomatoes, but the beans should be fresh.

3 cloves garlic, minced
3-4 shallots, chopped
2 tbs. olive oil
1½ lb. thin green beans, ends trimmed
3-4 ripe Roma tomatoes, peeled
2 tbs. lemon juice
salt and pepper to taste
2 tbs. chopped fresh dill

In a small skillet, sauté garlic and shallots in oil over medium heat until limp, about 3 minutes. Add beans, tomatoes, lemon juice, salt and pepper and simmer until beans are tender, about 5 minutes. Cooking time will depend on the tenderness of beans. Add chopped dill and serve immediately.

STEWED OKRA

This is a simple side dish that goes with lamb or a pilaf. Fresh okra is better, but frozen okra can be used in this recipe.

1½ lb. small fresh okra, rinsed just before using,
   or 2 pkg. (10 oz. each) frozen okra, thawed
3 tbs. butter
1 tbs. olive oil
1 large onion, thinly sliced
1 can (8 oz.) tomato sauce
½ cup water
salt and pepper to taste

Cut off cone-shaped layer from okra, removing stems. Heat butter and oil in a large saucepan over medium heat until bubbly. Add onion and sauté until limp. Add okra, tomato sauce, water, salt and pepper. Cover and cook over low heat for about 30 minutes, or until okra is tender, stirring occasionally. Serve hot.

OKRA AND RICE

If you've always wanted to try okra, this is a good way to start. It combines beautifully with any kind of cooked rice or a mixture of white rice, brown rice and/or wild rice. Buy okra just before using; it doesn't store well. Look for a bright green color; the okra pods should be no more than 3 inches long.

1½ cups rice
3½ cups water, chicken stock or vegetable stock
1 lb. fresh okra, rinsed just before using
3 tbs. butter
3 tbs. vegetable oil
1 cup chopped onion
1 tbs. grated fresh ginger
1 tsp. curry powder, or more to taste
¼ cup lemon juice
salt and pepper to taste

Cook rice according to package directions in water or broth; cool slightly. Remove cone-shaped layer from okra and cut okra into ½-inch slices. Combine butter and oil in a large skillet over medium heat and heat until bubbly. Add okra, onion and ginger and sauté until okra is barely tender, about 8 to 10 minutes. Stir in curry powder, lemon juice, salt and pepper and continue cooking for a few more minutes. Combine with cooked rice and mix well over low heat until heated through. Serve immediately.

POTATO AND SWEET PEPPER GRATIN

Here's a knock-your-socks-off potato dish that is visually appealing and goes with any meat dish, or it can be used as a vegetarian offering. This dish can be prepared in advance and reheated at the last minute. To save time, slice the potatoes with a food processor.

2½ lb. baking potatoes, peeled, cut into ¼-inch slices
2 large red and/or yellow bell peppers, cut into ¼-inch strips
1 tsp. mixed dried Italian herbs, or more to taste
salt and pepper to taste
½ cup grated imported Parmesan cheese, or more to taste
½ cup dry white wine
½ cup chicken stock
3 tbs. olive oil

Heat oven to 375°. Grease a large baking dish with olive oil. Place ⅓ of the potatoes in overlapping rows in dish. Place ½ of the peppers over potatoes. Sprinkle with ½ tsp. of the herbs, salt and pepper. Sprinkle ½ of the cheese over vegetables. Repeat layers. Top with remaining ⅓ of the potatoes. Combine wine and stock and pour over vegetables. Drizzle vegetables with olive oil. Cover dish with aluminum foil and bake for about 45 minutes. Remove foil, add more herbs, salt, pepper and cheese, if desired, and bake until potatoes can be easily pierced with a fork and the top is brown about 10 minutes. Remove dish from oven and serve immediately.

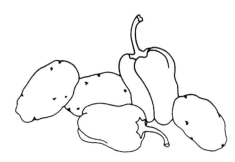

POTATO AND ZUCCHINI FRITTATA

This is a never-fail brunch recipe as well as a hearty side dish. A food processor makes preparation almost instant. This frittata is good warm or cold.

3 large baking potatoes, peeled
1 large zucchini
1 medium onion
3 eggs, lightly beaten
1/2 cup seasoned dry breadcrumbs
salt and pepper to taste
2 tbs. chopped fresh dill, or 1 tsp. dried, optional
vegetable oil for frying

Grate potatoes, zucchini and onion and mix together. Squeeze moisture out of mixture with your hands and place in a bowl. Add remaining ingredients, except oil, and mix thoroughly. Heat enough oil to coat the bottom of a 10- or 12-inch skillet over medium heat. Add 1/2 of the vegetable mixture, fry until golden brown and flip to brown the other side. Remove frittata from skillet and keep warm. Repeat with remaining mixture. Slice into wedges and serve at once.

SPINACH TART

This simple version of quiche has no crust. It is a great brunch dish and travels well. Use fresh spinach if it has been thoroughly washed and dried; otherwise, use frozen spinach. What you don't want is sand in your tart.

3 tbs. butter
1 cup chopped onion
¾ cup thinly sliced portobello or other mushrooms
2 lb. fresh spinach, stems removed, chopped,
   or 2 pkg. (10 oz. each) frozen chopped
   spinach, thawed, squeezed very dry
4 eggs, lightly beaten
1 cup shredded sharp cheddar cheese, or more to taste
1 tsp. Worcestershire sauce
salt and pepper to taste
½ tsp. nutmeg

Heat oven to 350°. Melt butter in a skillet over medium heat. Sauté onion and mushrooms until soft, about 3 to 4 minutes. Mix remaining ingredients in a bowl, add onion and mushroom mixture and pour into a lightly greased 10-inch quiche pan or a 9-inch square pan. Bake tart for about 45 minutes, or until eggs are set. Cut into wedges and serve hot or cold.

EGGS IN A SPINACH NEST

Servings: 6-8

This is a simple brunch dish that can be low in calories. Fresh spinach is preferred, but it needs more preparation time; frozen spinach is almost as good. If you want a richer combination, substitute part sour cream for the yogurt.

3 tbs. butter
1 large onion, chopped
2 lb. fresh spinach, thoroughly washed and dried, stems removed, chopped, or
   2 pkg. (10 oz. each) frozen leaf spinach, thawed, squeezed very dry
salt and pepper to taste
8 eggs
1 cup thick plain yogurt
1 clove garlic, finely chopped
½ cup grated Parmesan cheese
1 tbs. chopped fresh dill

Heat oven to 375°. Melt butter in a skillet over medium heat and sauté onion until limp. Combine onion with spinach, salt and pepper. Pat spinach mixture evenly into a 9-x-13-x-2-inch pan. Make a "nest" for each egg using the back of a spoon. Crack 1 egg into each nest, taking care not to break the yolk. Combine yogurt, garlic, cheese and dill and pour over spinach and eggs. Bake for about 20 minutes, until eggs are set. Serve immediately.

SPINACH YOGURT DIP

This is a wonderful dip for crackers, vegetables or rounds of French bread. Use fresh spinach if you are certain that there is no sand in it; frozen spinach tastes almost as good. For a special presentation, this can be served in a hollowed-out loaf of bread. It is important to drain the yogurt well in a mesh strainer to achieve the proper texture.

$\frac{1}{2}$ tbs. vegetable oil
2-3 cloves garlic, minced
$\frac{1}{2}$ red onion, finely chopped
1 lb. fresh spinach, thoroughly washed and dried, stems removed,
   or 1 pkg. (10 oz.) frozen chopped spinach, thawed, squeezed very dry
2 cups yogurt, well drained
1 tsp. dry mustard
salt and pepper to taste
$\frac{1}{2}$ tsp. sugar
$\frac{1}{4}$ cup sliced water chestnuts, well drained, chopped if pieces seem too large
$\frac{1}{2}$ cup grated Parmesan cheese

In a skillet, heat oil over medium heat. Sauté garlic and onion until limp. Add spinach and mix well. Transfer to a bowl, add remaining ingredients and mix well. Refrigerate until well chilled.

SPINACH PANCAKES

This is an adaptation of my mother's old recipe. It's a treat hot or cold, or it can be used as a sandwich filling in pita bread. It is an excellent introduction to spinach for non-spinach eaters. It's also excellent as a side dish for chicken, fish or anything else. A food processor takes just a minute to chop the spinach.

1½ lb. fresh spinach, thoroughly washed and dried
½ cup chopped green onions, with some of the green tops
¼ cup vegetable oil, plus more for frying
3 eggs, lightly beaten

¾ cup biscuit mix, or more if needed
½ cup grated Parmesan cheese
salt and pepper to taste
1 tsp. dried dill
1 tsp. dried chives
1 tsp. dried oregano

Coarsely chop spinach; use some of the stems if they are not too tough. Mix all ingredients, except frying oil, in a bowl. If mixture seems too loose, add a little more biscuit mix. Heat enough oil to coat the bottom of a large skillet over medium heat. With your hands, form spinach mixture into small pancakes and drop into hot oil. Fry pancakes until golden brown on one side. Flip to brown the other side. Drain on paper towels and serve immediately.

SAUTÉED CHERRY TOMATOES

The trick here is to use firm tomatoes. If they are soft to the touch, the tomatoes will fall apart. These tomatoes can also be used as a garnish for meat, chicken or other entrées.

¼ cup butter
1 qt. or more cherry tomatoes, stems removed
1 tsp. sugar, or less to taste
salt and pepper to taste
chopped fresh flat-leaf parsley, dill, chives or a combination to taste

Heat butter in a large skillet until bubbly. Add tomatoes and sugar and toss over high heat for about 2 to 3 minutes, shaking skillet constantly, until tomatoes are slightly cooked and shiny. Add salt, pepper and parsley and serve immediately.

FRIED GREEN TOMATOES AND NOODLES

Servings: 4-6

This combination is very satisfying. It is an easy summer dish when unripe tomatoes can be picked fresh from the garden. Any broad pasta, such as lasagna, works well. The recipe calls for Parmesan cheese, but other hard grating cheeses, such as Asiago or dry Jack, can be substituted.

1 lb. dried broad noodles
2 lb. green tomatoes, sliced about 1/2-inch thick
1/2 cup fine cornmeal
salt and pepper to taste
vegetable oil for frying
3-4 cloves garlic, finely chopped
1/4 cup olive oil
1/2 cup chopped fresh flat-leaf parsley
2-3 tbs. chopped fresh basil
grated Parmesan cheese for garnish

Cook noodles in a large amount of boiling salted water until slightly firm to the bite, *al dente*; do not overcook. Drain noodles and keep warm. Coat tomatoes with cornmeal, salt and pepper. Heat enough oil to coat the bottom of a large skillet over medium heat and sauté garlic until limp. Fry tomatoes in oil until browned, but not soft, about 6 to 8 minutes on each side; drain on paper towels. In a wide serving bowl, combine olive oil, parsley and basil. Add warm noodles and toss to coat thoroughly. Combine lightly with tomatoes and cheese and serve immediately.

TOMATO AND BREAD SALAD (PANZANELLA)

This simple salad can be a special treat, but unless you make it with delicious summer tomatoes and wonderful rustic Italian bread, don't bother.

5 tbs. extra virgin olive oil
2 tbs. red wine vinegar
1 tbs. balsamic vinegar
3-4 tbs. finely chopped red onion
1 tsp. finely chopped garlic, or more to taste
3 ripe tomatoes, cut into cubes
3-4 cups day-old Italian bread, cut into small cubes
1/4 cup chopped fresh basil, or more to taste
salt and pepper to taste

Combine oil and vinegars with onion and garlic. Let stand at room temperature for about 1 hour.

About 15 minutes before serving, combine remaining ingredients in a large bowl. Toss with dressing until bread has absorbed liquid. Serve immediately.

COLD TOMATO-BORSCHT SOUP

Servings: 6

The lovely pink color is just one of the pleasing elements of this easy icy cold summer soup — there's also nothing to cook! It should be prepared a day in advance to give the flavors a chance to blend thoroughly. Serve the soup with sliced dark bread.

2 cups tomato juice or vegetable juice, such as V-8
2 cups purchased borscht (Russian beet soup)
2 tbs. lemon juice
salt and pepper to taste
2 cups buttermilk
½ cup heavy cream
2 green onions, finely chopped
2 tbs. chopped fresh chives
chopped celery for garnish
chopped peeled and seeded cucumber for garnish
chopped hard-cooked egg for garnish, optional

Mix together all ingredients, except garnishes. Cover and let stand in the refrigerator for at least 24 hours. When ready to serve, sprinkle with celery, cucumber and chopped egg, if using.

SAUTÉ OF SUMMER SQUASH AND PEPPERS

Servings: 6-8

Here's a great summer dish for the times when you are awash with squash. It goes with just about anything and can be served cold. Using both dried and fresh herbs intensifies the herbal flavor.

3 tbs. olive oil
1 onion, chopped
1 clove garlic, minced
1 red bell pepper, cut into chunks
1 green bell pepper, cut into chunks
1 yellow bell pepper, cut into chunks
1 large zucchini, sliced
1 yellow crookneck squash, sliced
salt and pepper to taste
1 tsp. mixed dried mint, marjoram and
   parsley, or more to taste
chopped fresh herbs for garnish, optional

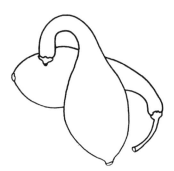

In a large skillet, heat oil over medium heat. Add onion and garlic and sauté until limp, about 3 minutes. Add remaining ingredients, except fresh herbs, and sauté until vegetables are tender-crisp, about 8 to 10 minutes. Top with fresh herbs, if using, and serve immediately.

ZUCCHINI FETA PANCAKES

The trick here is to dry the zucchini thoroughly; use your hands to squeeze out the moisture. Add a grated carrot for extra color.

4 cups grated zucchini, packed
4 eggs, separated
1 cup finely crumbled feta cheese
½ cup minced green onions
2 tbs. chopped fresh mint, or
   ¾ tsp. dried

2 tbs. chopped fresh dill, or
   ¾ tsp. dried
⅓ cup flour, plus more if needed
salt and pepper to taste
3 tbs. butter
sour cream or plain yogurt

With your hands, squeeze zucchini very dry and place in a large bowl. Lightly beat egg yolks and combine with zucchini, feta cheese, green onions, mint, dill, flour, salt and pepper. Beat egg whites until soft peaks form and fold into zucchini mixture. Melt butter in a large skillet over medium heat until bubbly. With your hands, form zucchini mixture into small pancakes and drop into hot butter. Fry pancakes until golden brown and crisp on one side. Flip to brown the other side. Drain on paper towels and serve immediately topped with sour cream or yogurt.

CURRIED ZUCCHINI SOUP
WITH CILANTRO

Servings: 6-8

This is a simple, satisfying soup, which looks and tastes much richer than it is. There is no cream or flour; the thickening is provided by a potato.

2 tbs. olive oil
1 medium onion, chopped
1 large potato, peeled, sliced
3 cloves garlic, minced
2 lb. zucchini, peeled if desired, sliced
1 tbs. curry powder, or to taste
3 cups chicken stock
1/4 cup minced fresh cilantro, or more to taste
salt and pepper to taste
1 qt. buttermilk
plain low-fat yogurt for garnish
lime wedges for garnish
cilantro sprigs for garnish

In a large saucepan, heat olive oil over medium heat. Add onion, potato and garlic and sauté until onion is limp, about 5 minutes. Add zucchini, curry powder, chicken stock, cilantro, salt and pepper. Bring to a boil, reduce heat to low, cover and simmer for 10 minutes. Add buttermilk and simmer for 5 minutes, or until potato and zucchini are tender. Puree soup with a food processor, return to pan and heat until very hot, but not boiling. Serve each portion with a dollop of yogurt, lime wedge and cilantro sprig.

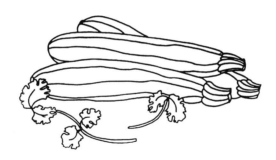

ZUCCHINI RICE BAKE

This is an all-purpose vegetable and rice dish to accompany chicken or meats. Or, it can be a vegetarian meal. Leftovers make a filling lunch.

1/4 cup olive oil
1 clove garlic, finely chopped
1 large onion, chopped
1 1/2 lb. zucchini, peeled if outer skin is tough, thinly sliced
salt and pepper to taste
2 cups milk
1 cup seasoned dry breadcrumbs
3 eggs, lightly beaten
1/2 tsp. mixed dried Italian herbs, or more to taste
3/4 cup grated Parmesan cheese
1/2 cup long-grain rice

In a skillet, heat 2 tbs. of the olive oil over medium heat. Add garlic and onion and sauté until limp. Add zucchini, salt and pepper and sauté for 5 minutes. Remove from heat. Heat oven to 350°. In large bowl, pour 1 cup of the milk over breadcrumbs. Add remaining 2 tbs. oil, eggs, herbs and ⅔ cup of the cheese. Add zucchini mixture and rice to bowl, mix well and transfer to an oiled gratin dish. Pour remaining milk and Parmesan over the top and bake for 1 hour, until eggs are set.

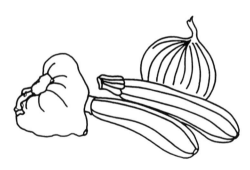

CREAMY BROCCOLI AND ZUCCHINI

Servings: 6-8

Quick to fix, this is a satisfying main dish. It can even be prepared ahead of time.

½ lb. spinach noodles
1 large bunch broccoli, trimmed, thick
   stalks peeled and sliced, tops cut
   into 2-inch florets
1 lb. zucchini, coarsely chopped
2 tbs. butter
1 medium onion, chopped
2 cloves garlic, minced

2 tbs. flour
salt and pepper to taste
1 tsp. mixed dried Italian herbs
1 cup milk
1 cup ricotta cheese or small curd
   cottage cheese
grated Parmesan cheese for topping

Cook noodles in a large amount of boiling salted water until slightly firm to the bite, *al dente*; drain and keep warm. Steam broccoli and zucchini until barely done, about 6 to 8 minutes. Melt butter in a large skillet over medium heat and sauté onion and garlic until limp. Add flour, salt, pepper and herbs and stir until thick. Slowly add milk and stir until thickened. Add ricotta and stir until nearly incorporated. Stir in broccoli and zucchini and mix well. Serve vegetable mixture over warm noodles and top with Parmesan cheese.

BROCCOLI AND GREEN PEAS

Servings: 6

These common vegetables combine to make a rather elegant dish. The tiny peas add a special touch.

2 tbs. butter
1/4 cup water
1 1/2 lb. broccoli, trimmed, stalks peeled and sliced, tops cut into small florets
1 pkg. (10 oz.) frozen petite peas, thawed
1/2 cup sliced green onions, with some of the green tops
2 tbs. lemon juice
salt and pepper to taste
1/4 cup chopped fresh flat-leaf parsley or dill

Melt butter in a large skillet over medium-high heat. Add water and broccoli stalks and sauté for about 3 to 5 minutes, until almost tender. Add broccoli florets, peas and green onions and cook for 2 minutes, stirring occasionally. Vegetables should be tender-crisp. Stir in lemon juice, salt, pepper and parsley. Serve hot.

POTATOES, BROCCOLI AND TOMATOES

This combination of ordinary vegetables makes a visually appealing side dish or a vegetarian lunch. It can be served hot or at room temperature.

2 lb. potatoes, peeled, cut into 1-inch chunks
2 cups water
salt to taste
1 large bunch broccoli, about 2 lb.
1 tbs. olive oil
1 tbs. butter
1 tbs. minced garlic
3-4 Roma tomatoes, cut in half, or 1 cup cherry tomatoes
salt and pepper to taste
3 tbs. grated Parmesan cheese

Combine potatoes, water and salt in large saucepan and cook until potatoes are tender, about 10 minutes; drain and set aside. Peel and trim broccoli stalks and cut into 2-inch pieces. Cut broccoli tops into 2-inch florets.

Heat olive oil and butter in a large skillet over medium heat. Add garlic and sauté for 1 minute. Increase heat to medium-high, add broccoli stalks and stir-fry for 3 minutes. Add broccoli florets and stir-fry for about 5 minutes. Add tomatoes, salt and pepper and stir-fry for about 3 minutes. Add cooked potatoes and stir-fry until heated through. Add a little water if mixture seems too dry. Correct seasonings. Top mixture with cheese and serve.

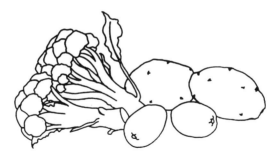

BROCCOLI WITH MUSHROOMS

This recipe has been updated to use wild mushrooms rather than white mushrooms. You can mix or substitute one for another if desired.

2 tbs. olive oil
2 tbs. butter
2-3 cloves garlic, finely minced
1 large bunch broccoli, trimmed, thick stalks
    peeled and sliced, tops cut into 2-inch florets
1-2 cups sliced portobello, shiitake or white mushrooms
salt and pepper to taste
2 tbs. lemon juice
2 tbs. chopped fresh dill
3-4 green onions, chopped

In a large saucepan, heat oil and butter over medium-high heat. Add garlic and broccoli stalks and sauté for about 5 minutes, until broccoli is almost tender. Add broccoli florets and mushrooms and cook for 5 minutes, until broccoli is tender-crisp. Remove from heat and add salt, pepper, lemon juice, dill and green onions. Serve at once.

SWEET ONION BAKE

Slice the onions with a food processor; it's easier on the eyes. This dish is a great go-with for fish; add a salad and dinner is ready. Look for sweet, mild Vidalia onions in specialty markets during May and June.

1 cup water
$\frac{1}{2}$ tsp. salt
$\frac{1}{2}$ cup long-grain rice
$\frac{1}{4}$ cup butter
6 cups sliced sweet onions, Vidalia preferred
$\frac{3}{4}$ cup grated Gruyère or Swiss cheese
$\frac{3}{4}$ cup half-and-half, or less to taste
salt and pepper to taste

In a saucepan, combine water, salt and rice. Bring to a rolling boil, cover and immediately reduce heat to the lowest setting. Cook rice until just done, no more than 15 minutes. Heat oven to 300°. In a large skillet, melt butter over medium heat and sauté onions until limp. Combine sautéed onions and cooked rice with remaining ingredients in a baking dish. Cover and bake for about 1 hour, until onions are very tender. Serve at once.

FRIED SWEET ONIONS AND EGGS

Servings: 6-8

This is very a simple, comforting dish, but you should slice the onions in a food processor to spare your eyes from crying. Vidalia onions, a special variety of sweet onions from Vidalia, Georgia, are a special treat. They are available only in the months of May and June. Look for them in specialty supermarkets, or they can be ordered through the mail. The optional sugar helps to brown the onions to a nice caramel color.

1/4 cup vegetable oil
6 cups sliced sweet onions, or more to taste
1 tsp. sugar, optional
8 eggs
salt and pepper to taste
1/4 cup water

Heat oil in a large skillet over medium heat until very hot. Add onions to skillet all at once with sugar, if using, and cook until some liquid forms on the bottom of skillet. Stir thoroughly. Cook mixture for about 20 minutes, stirring often, until evenly browned. At the end of cooking time, onions should be about 1/3 the original volume and very brown.

In a bowl, beat eggs until frothy. Add salt, pepper and water to bowl and mix well. Pour egg mixture over onions and cook until eggs just begin to set. Continue to cook, stirring frequently, until eggs are scrambled and mixed well with onions. Serve immediately.

VEGETABLE DISHES FOR FALL AND WINTER

BAKED CAULIFLOWER
WITH CAPERS AND OLIVES

Baking cauliflower, or other vegetables, intensifies the flavor. This dish can be prepared ahead of time and is a lovely accompaniment to fish.

1 head cauliflower, about 2 lb., cut into florets
1 tsp. salt
about 1 tbs. olive oil
¼ cup butter
½ cup minced shallots or green onions
1 large clove garlic, minced
2 tbs. drained small capers
2 tbs. chopped kalamata olives
salt and pepper to taste
3 tbs. dried breadcrumbs
2 tbs. chopped fresh flat-leaf parsley

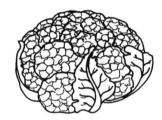

Heat oven to 375°. Place cauliflower in a large saucepan and cover with water. Add salt, bring to a boil and boil for about 3 minutes; drain. Place cauliflower in a baking dish and toss with olive oil. Place in oven and bake for about 15 minutes.

Melt butter in a large skillet over medium heat. Add shallots and garlic and sauté until softened. Add capers and olives and cook for 1 minute. Add salt and pepper. Place caper-olive mixture on top of cauliflower and top with breadcrumbs that have been mixed with parsley. Return to oven and bake for 15 to 20 minutes, until cauliflower is easily pierced with a knife. Serve immediately or save for later use. Reheat for 15 minutes, until warmed through.

CAULIFLOWER WITH
CURRIED YOGURT SAUCE

There is no curry powder in this recipe. The combination of spices gives the dish the Indian flavor. The sauce can be used for other mild-flavored vegetables, such as potatoes or peas.

1 large head cauliflower, about 2 lb., cut into florets
1 tbs. vegetable oil
1 large onion, finely chopped
1½ cups plain yogurt
1 tsp. ground cumin, or more to taste
1 tsp. ground coriander, or more to taste
½ tsp. turmeric
⅛ tsp. cayenne pepper, or more to taste
salt and pepper to taste
chopped fresh cilantro for garnish

Steam cauliflower florets until just tender, about 15 to 20 minutes; drain and keep warm. In a small skillet, heat oil over medium-high heat and sauté onion until tender and golden. Add a little water, if necessary, to prevent sticking. Reduce heat to low. Combine yogurt with seasonings and add to skillet with onion. Simmer for a few minutes and mix well; sauce should not boil. Place cauliflower in a serving dish and top with sauce. Sprinkle with fresh cilantro and serve immediately.

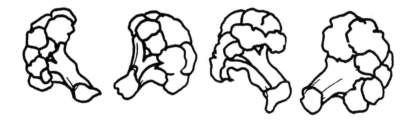

BRUSSELS SPROUTS WITH BACON AND ROASTED PEPPERS

Servings: 6-8

If you think you don't like Brussels sprouts, try this dish. It's a mind-changer. The bacon can be omitted, but it adds a special taste to the dish. You can use purchased roasted red peppers if desired.

1½ lb. Brussels sprouts, small size preferred
1 tbs. butter
2 tbs. olive oil
½ cup chopped mushrooms
2 shallots, minced
¼ cup chopped red onion
1 small red bell pepper, roasted, peeled, seeded, chopped
2 tbs. minced fresh flat-leaf parsley
3-4 tbs. balsamic vinegar
salt and pepper to taste
¼ lb. bacon, diced and cooked until crisp, optional

Trim Brussels sprouts and remove outer leaves. If they are large, use a knife to form an X on the stem end of each sprout. Steam Brussels sprouts for about 8 to 10 minutes, or until just tender-crisp; drain and set aside. In a skillet, heat butter and olive oil over medium heat until bubbly. Sauté mushrooms and shallots for a few minutes. Add red onion and sauté briefly to blend. Add red pepper, parsley, balsamic vinegar, salt and pepper. Add sprouts and bacon, if using, and heat for a few minutes. Serve immediately.

MARINATED BRUSSELS SPROUTS

Servings: 6

Make more of this dish than you think you will need. It has a way of disappearing before serving time. Everyone who opens the refrigerator door has to taste "just one." Try to use Brussels sprouts that are similar in size.

2 lb. Brussels sprouts, small size preferred
½ cup tarragon-flavored white wine vinegar
½ cup olive oil
3 cloves garlic, finely chopped, or more to taste
1 tsp. Dijon mustard, or more to taste
1 tbs. mixed dried Italian herbs
½ tbs. sugar
salt and pepper to taste
dash hot pepper sauce
3-4 green onions, chopped

Trim Brussels sprouts and remove outer leaves. Cut a small X on the stem end of each sprout. Steam Brussels sprouts for about 8 to 10 minutes, or until just tender-crisp; drain and keep warm. Mix together remaining ingredients and pour over sprouts. Place in a locking plastic bag and marinate in the refrigerator for 1 to 3 days. Serve at room temperature.

GARLICKY BROCCOLI RABE

Broccoli rabe is not the same as broccoli; it is a leafy green vegetable related to cabbage and has a slightly bitter flavor. Look for small, broccoli-like florets on long edible stalks. Broccoli rabe is easy to prepare and is delicious served hot or at room temperature. You can toast the breadcrumbs in advance to save time.

3 tbs. olive oil
2 cloves garlic, finely minced
1 cup dry breadcrumbs
1 lb. or more broccoli rabe,
   tough stems removed
1 clove garlic, finely minced
salt and pepper to taste
3 tbs. lemon juice

Heat olive oil in a skillet over low heat and add 2 cloves minced garlic and breadcrumbs. Sauté until breadcrumbs are toasted, about 5 minutes; cool. Steam broccoli rabe for about 5 minutes, until tender-crisp; drain and place in a serving bowl. Add 1 clove minced garlic, salt, pepper and lemon juice to bowl and stir until mixed. Top with garlic breadcrumbs and serve.

DUTCH RED CABBAGE

Red cabbage seems more special than ordinary green cabbage. This is an old recipe that has been simplified for easy preparation. The shredding can be done almost instantly with a food processor.

½ cup chopped onion
2 tbs. butter
5-6 cups shredded red cabbage
1½ cups diced green apples
5 whole cloves
salt and pepper to taste
1 tsp. sugar
2 tbs. red wine vinegar
½ cup water

In a large saucepan, sauté onion in butter over medium heat until limp. Add remaining ingredients. Cover pan, reduce heat to low and cook for about 15 minutes, stirring occasionally, until cabbage is tender.

SWEET-AND-SOUR CABBAGE

Cabbage is a reliable standby. It's a vegetable that can be stored in the refrigerator for a week or more. This simple cabbage preparation goes with any roasted meat or chicken dish.

2 tbs. cider vinegar
2 tbs. water
1 tbs. sugar, or more to taste
2 tbs. soy sauce
salt and pepper to taste
$\frac{1}{4}$ cup vegetable oil
1 medium head red cabbage, cored, cut into $\frac{1}{4}$-inch strips

In a small bowl, combine vinegar, water, sugar, soy sauce, salt and pepper; set aside. Heat oil in a large skillet over medium-high heat. Add cabbage and stir-fry until tender-crisp, about 5 to 6 minutes. Stir in vinegar mixture and cook, stirring constantly, until cabbage is tender, about 3 minutes. Serve immediately.

CABBAGE NOODLES

This quick-to-prepare, old-fashioned cabbage and noodle dish goes with many meat dishes. Served by itself, it makes a great lunch.

1 lb. egg noodles
2-3 lb. green cabbage, cored, shredded
about 1 tbs. kosher salt
1/4 cup vegetable oil, or more if needed
1/4 cup butter, or more if needed
salt and pepper to taste
chopped fresh flat-leaf parsley for garnish

Cook noodles in a large amount of boiling salted water until slightly firm to the bite, *al dente*; drain. Place shredded cabbage in a colander and sprinkle with salt. Place a weight on top of cabbage and let stand in a bowl or over the sink for 10 minutes or more. In a large skillet, heat oil and butter over medium-high heat until bubbly. Add 1/2 of the cabbage to skillet and sauté until tender-crisp. Stir in remaining cabbage and continue cooking for about 15 minutes, until cabbage is cooked. Add more oil and butter if needed. Mix in cooked noodles and heat through. Season with salt and pepper. Place in a large bowl, top with chopped parsley and serve.

PICKLED BEETS

This old-time relish goes with many dishes and always looks lovely on the table. Although fresh beets are preferable in this recipe, canned beets will work as well.

2 lb. fresh whole baby beets, scrubbed, or canned whole baby beets
2 cups cider vinegar
¾ cup sugar
½ tsp. salt
1 tsp. pickling spice
3 bay leaves
1 onion, thinly sliced, separated into rings

Place fresh beets in a saucepan and cover with water. Bring to a boil, reduce heat to medium-low and simmer for 20 to 25 minutes, until tender when pierced with a knife; drain. Remove peels with a small paring knife. Combine vinegar, sugar and salt in a nonaluminum saucepan. Tie pickling spice in a cheesecloth bag and add to vinegar mixture with bay leaves. Bring to a boil, add cooked beets and onion and bring back to a boil. Boil for 2 minutes. Remove pan from heat and let beets stand in liquid until cooled. Remove cheesecloth bag and bay leaves. Place beets, onions and enough marinade to cover into a glass bowl. Refrigerate overnight before serving.

BAKED BEETS WITH YOGURT

Servings: 6

This is a simple way to serve beets — they need no peeling and no boiling. Bake them as you would a potato.

6 large beets, scrubbed, trimmed
1½ cups plain yogurt
salt and pepper to taste
1 tbs. minced fresh dill, or more to taste
¼ cup chopped fresh chives

Heat oven to 425°. Pierce beets with a fork several times. Place beets on a rack in oven and bake until tender, about 1 hour; cool. Mix together remaining ingredients. With a paring knife, slip off skins from cooled beets. Slice or quarter beets, place in a serving bowl and top with yogurt sauce. Serve warm or at room temperature.

ROASTED FENNEL

If you haven't yet tried this licorice-flavored vegetable, this is a simple, foolproof way to make it. The feathery fronds can be snipped and added to a salad for an interesting taste.

4 medium bulbs fennel, quartered, cored
2 tbs. olive oil
salt and pepper to taste
2 tbs. chopped fresh flat-leaf parsley

Heat oven to 425°. Toss fennel with olive oil and season with salt and pepper. Place in a roasting pan just large enough to hold bulbs in a single layer. Roast for about 35 to 40 minutes, turning once or twice. Fennel should be golden brown and tender. Sprinkle with parsley and serve.

LEEK AND FENNEL GRATIN

This sounds like an unusual combination, but it is surprisingly good. It is a nice companion to roasted or grilled meat or even broiled fish. Heavy cream can be substituted for yogurt, if you're not counting calories.

2 large bulbs fennel, about 2½ lb.
3 medium leeks, white part and a small amount of the green part only
½ cup plain yogurt
½ cup grated Parmesan cheese
¼ tsp. nutmeg
salt and pepper to taste
2 tbs. dried breadcrumbs
2 tbs. grated Parmesan cheese
2 tbs. butter
fennel fronds for garnish

Heat oven to 350°. Cut fennel bulbs into quarters. Cut away most of the tough core. Cut quarters into ½-inch strips. Cut trimmed leeks in half lengthwise; cut crosswise into ½-inch slices. Place leek slices in a large bowl of cold water, separating to remove any sand between the layers and swishing in water until no sand remains. Drain and dry leeks. Combine chopped fennel, leeks, yogurt, ½ cup Parmesan, nutmeg, salt and pepper in a 1½-quart baking dish. Mix well. Combine 2 tbs. breadcrumbs with 2 tbs. Parmesan and sprinkle over the top. Dot with butter. Bake for about 45 minutes, until fennel is tender and top is browned. Garnish with fennel fronds. Serve hot.

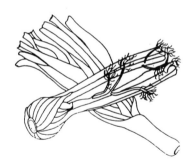

LEEK FRITTATA

This is yet another variation of the classic Italian omelet. It makes a satisfying brunch dish, or add a salad for a complete lunch. Chèvre (soft white goat cheese) adds a unique flavor. Another soft, flavorful cheese can be substituted, but chèvre is preferred.

10 medium leeks, root ends and dark green portions removed
1/4 cup butter
2 tbs. olive oil
2 tbs. lemon juice
1 tsp. sugar
8 eggs
2 oz. chèvre, or more to taste, cut into small pieces
1/4 cup chopped fresh dill, optional
salt and pepper to taste
4-6 oz. cream cheese, cut into small pieces
chopped fresh flat-leaf parsley for garnish

Rinse leeks thoroughly. Cut white part and a small part of the green part into ¼-inch slices. Soak slices in cold water for about 30 minutes to be sure all sand has been removed. Drain and pat dry. Heat butter and olive oil in a 12-inch ovenproof skillet over medium-high heat. Add leeks and sauté until wilted. Stir in lemon juice and sugar. Reduce heat to low and simmer until very tender, about 20 minutes. Heat broiler. With a wire whisk, beat eggs, chèvre, dill, if using, salt and pepper in a bowl. Pour into skillet and cook over low heat until bottom of eggs is just set. Dot with cream cheese and place under broiler. Broil just until top is slightly brown, about 2 minutes, watching carefully. Sprinkle with chopped parsley and serve.

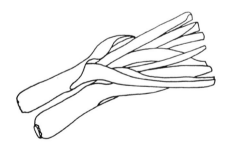

CARROTS AND BULGUR

Servings: 6

This is a good side dish or vegetarian main dish. Add a salad and a loaf of bread and you've got a complete meal. Look for bulgur wheat in the bulk bins of your supermarket or in boxes on the shelf near the rice.

2 tbs. butter
1 large onion, chopped
1 lb. carrots, peeled, cut into 1/2-inch slices
1/2 tsp. cinnamon
1/2 tsp. cumin
salt and pepper to taste
1 cup bulgur wheat
1/3 cup raisins or dried currants
3 cups chicken stock or water
3-4 green onions, with some of the green tops, chopped
3 tbs. chopped fresh cilantro

Melt butter in a large saucepan over medium heat and sauté onion and carrots for 5 minutes. Add cinnamon, cumin, salt, pepper, bulgur, raisins and chicken stock and mix well. Cover and cook until carrots are tender-crisp and liquid is absorbed, about 15 minutes. Top with green onions and cilantro and serve.

CARROTS IN WHITE WINE

Here, simple carrots are transformed into something special. They should not be overcooked. Use baby carrots for a lovely presentation.

2 lb. carrots, peeled, cut into 1/4-inch-thick slices, or 2 lb. baby carrots
1 1/2 cups diced celery, including some of the leaves
1 large onion, chopped
1 cup dry white wine
2 tbs. sugar
1/4 cup butter
salt and pepper to taste
2-3 tbs. chopped fresh dill, or 1 tsp. dried

In a large saucepan, combine all ingredients, except dill. Cover and cook over low heat until carrots are just tender-crisp, about 6 to 8 minutes. Sprinkle with dill and serve.

SPICY CARROT SOUP

The lovely color adds to the enjoyment of this soup. Most of the preparation can be done a day in advance. Add the yogurt at the last minute.

2 tbs. butter
1 medium onion, coarsely chopped
2 leeks, white part only, coarsely chopped
1 lb. carrots, peeled, coarsely chopped
3 stalks celery, including some of the leaves, chopped
1 large potato, peeled, sliced
1 can (46 oz.) chicken broth
1½ cups unsweetened pineapple juice
2 tbs. light brown sugar
3 tbs. chopped fresh flat-leaf parsley
4-6 whole cloves
2 tsp. salt
½ tsp. ground white pepper
½ tsp. ground allspice
1 tsp. ground cumin, or more to taste
1 cup plain yogurt
chopped fresh parsley or cilantro for garnish

Melt butter in large saucepan over medium-high heat and sauté onion, leeks, carrots, celery and potato for a few minutes. Add broth, pineapple juice, sugar, 3 tbs. parsley, cloves, salt, pepper, allspice and cumin and sauté until vegetables are tender, about 20 minutes. Cool, remove cloves and puree mixture with a blender or food processor. Pour into a storage container, cover and refrigerate for up to 3 days. Just before serving, pour soup into a saucepan, add yogurt and heat gently until heated through; do not boil. Garnish with parsley and serve.

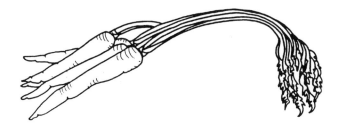

CARROTS MOROCCAN-STYLE

Servings: 6-8

A salad, a side-dish, an addition to a buffet table — this dish is a sleeper. No one expects it to taste so good. Use baby carrots for even easier preparation.

2 lb. carrots, peeled, cut into diagonal chunks, or 2 lb. baby carrots
1/2 cup olive oil
1/2 cup red wine vinegar
1 tsp. Dijon mustard
1/2 tsp. sugar
1 cup chopped fresh flat-leaf parsley
4 cloves garlic, finely chopped
1/2 tsp. ground cumin, or more to taste
1/2 tsp. paprika
salt and pepper to taste
3 green onions, with some of the green tops, chopped

Cook carrots in boiling salted water until still firm, about 4 to 8 minutes; drain and keep warm. Mix together remaining ingredients, except green onions, and pour over warm carrots in a bowl or locking plastic bag. Cover bowl and marinate carrots for up to 3 days in the refrigerator. Just before serving, sprinkle carrots with green onions. Serve cold or at room temperature.

BAKED PARSNIPS

Parsnips look a little like white carrots, but have a sweeter and more intense flavor. They go very well with any roasted meat.

2 lb. parsnips, peeled,
   cut into chunks
¼ cup vegetable oil
salt and pepper to taste
chopped fresh flat-leaf parsley
   or dill for garnish

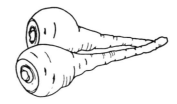

Heat oven to 425°. Place parsnips on a baking sheet and toss with oil. Season with salt and pepper. Bake for 15 to 20 minutes, depending on the size of parsnip pieces, turning once or twice. If you like them crisp, bake for a few minutes longer. Sprinkle with herbs and serve.

PARSNIPS WITH WATERCRESS

This is a simple dish that goes well with any broiled or roasted meat. Combine parsnips and carrots for an unusual vegetable offering.

6 medium parsnips, peeled, cut into 1/2-inch slices
1 large bunch watercress, washed thoroughly, tough stems removed
2 tbs. butter
6 shallots, finely chopped
2 large cloves garlic, finely minced
salt and pepper to taste
1/2 cup grated sharp cheddar cheese, or more to taste

Steam parsnips until tender, about 12 to 15 minutes; do not overcook; drain and keep warm. Steam watercress for 2 to 3 minutes; drain and keep warm.

Heat oven to 350°. Melt butter in a medium skillet over medium heat and sauté shallots and garlic until limp. Add parsnips, watercress, salt and pepper and mix well. Transfer mixture to a baking dish and top with cheddar cheese. Bake uncovered for about 10 minutes, until cheese melts and dish is thoroughly heated through. Serve immediately.

RUTABAGA AND WATERCRESS PUREE

This is a simple way to introduce rutabagas to your family. It is a delightful accompaniment to fish or poultry.

2 lb. rutabagas, peeled, cut
   into small chunks
1 large bunch watercress, washed
   thoroughly, tough stems removed
2 tbs. butter, melted
1/2 cup half-and-half or milk
salt and pepper to taste

Cook rutabagas in boiling salted water for about 30 minutes, until very tender; drain. With a food processor, puree rutabagas with 1/2 of the watercress until very smooth. Combine with butter, half-and-half, salt and pepper. Mix well and place in a saucepan. Heat over low heat, stirring until heated through. Top with remaining watercress and serve.

RUTABAGAS AU GRATIN

I have never heard anyone say, "Rutabagas are my favorite vegetable." Maybe it's hard to love anything called "rutabaga." But, prepared this way, they are really good eating.

2 lb. rutabagas, peeled, sliced
1/4 cup butter
1/4 cup flour
1 cup milk
1 tsp. mixed dried Italian herbs, or more to taste
salt and pepper to taste
1 cup grated sharp cheddar cheese
1/2 cup or more seasoned dried breadcrumbs
2 tbs. butter

Heat oven to 400°. In a 3-quart saucepan, boil rutabagas in salted water to cover for about 10 minutes; rutabagas should be underdone. Drain water from rutabagas. In a skillet, melt butter over medium heat. Add flour and stir until thick. Add milk, herbs, salt and pepper and stir until smooth and thick. Add cheese and stir until melted. Place rutabagas in a buttered 2-quart casserole. Pour cheese sauce over rutabagas. Combine breadcrumbs with butter and sprinkle over the top of sauce. Bake for about 15 minutes, until rutabagas are tender.

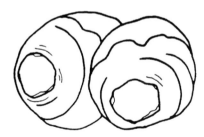

BAKED POTATOES AND RUTABAGAS

Servings: 6-8

After you peel the rutabagas and potatoes, this dish almost makes itself. It is a hearty go-with for roasted meats or chicken and is full of beta carotene, vitamin C and other good things. Yukon Gold potatoes are particularly tasty in this dish.

1 lb. rutabagas, peeled, cut into pieces
1½ lb. potatoes, peeled, cut into pieces
1-2 tbs. olive oil
2 eggs, lightly beaten
1 cup small-curd cottage cheese
1 cup shredded sharp cheddar cheese
1 tbs. minced fresh dill or tarragon
2 tbs. minced fresh chives
salt and pepper to taste

Heat oven to 375°. Combine rutabagas and potatoes in a large bowl and toss with olive oil. Place on a large baking sheet. Bake until vegetables can be pierced easily with a fork, about 20 to 30 minutes. Combine hot baked vegetables with remaining ingredients in a bowl. Pour into a food processor workbowl and process just until combined; do not overprocess or potatoes may become gummy. You may have to process mixture in 2 batches. Serve at once. Or, for a special treat, spread mixture in an oiled 9-inch square baking pan and bake at 350° until lightly browned, about 15 to 20 minutes. Let baked mixture stand for a few minutes before serving.

RUTABAGA-POTATO PUREE

Servings: 6-8

If you want to try rutabagas, this is a good recipe to use. The combination produces a very pleasant sweetness. It goes beautifully with roasted turkey or other meats. Parsnips or small turnips can be substituted for the rutabagas.

1 lb. rutabagas, peeled, cut into small chunks
1 lb. baking potatoes, peeled, cut into small chunks
1 tbs. butter or olive oil
salt and pepper to taste
½ tsp. nutmeg
2 tbs. chopped fresh dill or flat-leaf parsley

In a large saucepan, combine rutabagas and potatoes and add water to cover. Bring to a boil, reduce heat to low, cover and simmer until vegetables are tender, about 15 to 20 minutes. Drain vegetables. Mash vegetables with a potato masher or puree with a food processor just until combined; do not overprocess or potatoes may become gummy. Place in a serving dish with butter, salt, pepper, nutmeg and herbs; mix thoroughly. Serve immediately or keep warm until ready to serve.

CELERY ROOT AND POTATO PUREE

Servings: 6-8

Celery root is also known as celeriac. Pairing it with potatoes makes an unusual side dish. Though the combination looks like potatoes, it has a unique flavor.

2 lb. boiling potatoes, peeled,
   quartered
1 celery root, about 1 lb., peeled,
   cut into chunks
about ½ cup hot milk, cream or
   liquid from cooking celery root
butter to taste
salt and pepper to taste
1-2 cloves garlic, finely minced, optional
chopped fresh flat-leaf parsley or dill, optional

Cook potatoes and celery root separately in boiling salted water until very tender, about 10 to 15 minutes; drain. Mash vegetables together with a potato masher or food processor, adding milk, butter, salt, pepper and garlic, if using. Do not overprocess or mixture may become gummy. Stir in parsley if desired. Serve at once.

ROASTED POTATOES WITH WHITE WINE

Servings: 6-8

White wine gives these potatoes an unexpected flavor. Serve them with roasted meats or poultry.

6 large baking potatoes, peeled, cut into long wedges
3 tbs. olive oil
2 large cloves garlic, finely minced
1 tsp. mixed dried Italian herbs
1/2 tsp. paprika
salt and pepper to taste
1/2 cup dry white wine
chopped fresh flat-leaf parsley for garnish

Heat oven to 425°. Toss potato wedges with olive oil, garlic, herbs, paprika, salt and pepper. Place on a baking sheet and drizzle with white wine. Bake for about 25 to 30 minutes, until tender. Top with parsley and serve.

SWEET POTATO CHIPS

Servings: 3 or more

The problem with this recipe is that it is difficult to keep the chips from being eaten before you are ready to serve them. Children, as well as adults, love them. The thinnest slicing attachment for your food processor works fine for slicing the sweet potatoes.

3-4 long thin sweet potatoes, scrubbed
1 tbs. vegetable oil
1 tsp. cinnamon, or less to taste
½ tsp. salt
½ tsp. sugar, or less to taste

Heat oven to 425°. Cut sweet potatoes into very thin slices and toss with oil. Place oiled potatoes on a large baking sheet in a single layer. Sprinkle with remaining ingredients and bake until potatoes are brown, about 15 to 20 minutes, turning once with a spatula. Bake for a few minutes longer, watching carefully, until crisp. Serve hot or at room temperature.

COUSCOUS WITH SWEET POTATOES AND TURNIPS

This can be used as a main course or as a side dish for meat. The combination is unusual and hearty. Roasting the vegetables is easy and brings out their flavor.

¼ cup olive oil
4 cloves garlic, minced
6 medium turnips, peeled, quartered
3 medium sweet potatoes, peeled,
  thickly sliced
1 medium rutabaga, peeled,
  thinly sliced
3 cups couscous
¼ cup butter
1 bunch green onions, with some of the
  green tops, chopped

½ cup pine nuts, lightly toasted
½ cup dried currants
1½ cups pitted prunes
1 cup vegetable or chicken stock, or
  more if needed
2 tsp. ground cumin
½ tsp. cinnamon
¼ tsp. ground allspice
¼ tsp. nutmeg
salt and pepper to taste

Heat oven to 375°. In a large bowl, combine olive oil, minced garlic, turnips, sweet potatoes and rutabaga and toss to coat vegetables with oil. Place vegetables on a large baking sheet and bake until tender when pierced with a fork, about 45 minutes. While vegetables are baking, prepare couscous according to package directions. Mix in butter, green onions, pine nuts and currants. Return baked vegetables to bowl and add prunes, stock and spices; mix well. Mound couscous mixture on a platter and surround with vegetable mixture. Serve hot.

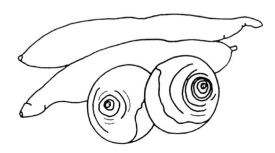

SWEET POTATO AND CASHEW CASSEROLE

Servings: 8

The difference between yams and sweet potatoes has blurred over the years. Look for the variety with dark orange, sweet flesh. Use long thin sweet potatoes; they bake more quickly. The nuts give these potatoes an unexpected crunch.

3 lb. long, thin sweet potatoes
1 tsp. cinnamon
salt and pepper to taste
1 egg, lightly beaten
1/3 cup pineapple juice

1/3 cup apple juice
1/4 cup sugar
3 tbs. butter, room temperature
1/2 cup coarsely chopped salted cashews

Heat oven to 350°. Scrub sweet potatoes and bake on oven rack until tender, about 35 to 40 minutes. Cut sweet potatoes in half, scoop out sweet potato flesh and place in a large bowl. With a potato masher, mash potato flesh until almost smooth. Add cinnamon, salt, pepper, egg, juices and sugar and beat with a spoon until fluffy. Beat in 2 tbs. of the butter. Spread potatoes in a shallow baking dish. Cover and refrigerate if making ahead. Shortly before serving, melt remaining 1 tbs. butter in a skillet and sauté cashews for about 3 minutes, until lightly browned. Sprinkle nuts over sweet potato mixture. Bake for about 20 minutes, until heated through.

OVEN-CANDIED SWEET POTATOES

Servings: 6-8

Start with raw sweet potatoes for this dish; the potatoes stay firm and caramelize to a golden color. Long thin potatoes are easier to handle. The dish can be prepared the day before serving and reheated when ready to eat. It goes well with turkey or any other poultry.

8 medium sweet potatoes, peeled
¼ cup butter
¾ cup brown sugar, packed
½ tsp. cinnamon
salt and pepper to taste
¼ cup orange juice
2 tsp. grated fresh orange peel (zest)

Heat oven to 400°. Halve sweet potatoes lengthwise. Melt butter in a large skillet over medium-high heat. Brown raw potatoes in butter on all sides. Place sweet potatoes with butter in a shallow baking dish. Add sugar and remaining ingredients. Cover with aluminum foil and bake for 30 minutes. Remove cover and bake for 20 minutes, basting often with pan juices, until potatoes are tender and golden. Serve hot.

BAKED PUMPKIN AND APPLES
WITH CINNAMON YOGURT SAUCE

This is a special fall dish; it is a great addition to the Thanksgiving table. The pumpkin can be cut in half or placed in the oven whole. The only caveat is that if you use a whole pumpkin, pierce it with a fork in several places to let the steam escape.

1 pumpkin, 2 lb. or more, whole or halved
2 large Granny Smith or other tart apples,
   peeled, cored, sliced
1/4 cup butter
1/4 cup sugar
salt and pepper to taste
1/2 cup blanched almonds or hazelnuts
1 cup plain yogurt
1 tsp. sugar
1 tsp. cinnamon
chopped fresh flat-leaf parsley for garnish

Heat oven to 375°. Place pumpkin on a baking sheet and bake for 1 hour, or until easily pierced with a fork. While pumpkin is baking, sauté apples in butter over medium heat until soft, about 5 minutes. Add 1/4 cup sugar, salt and pepper and cook for 2 minutes. Place nuts on a baking sheet and bake for about 5 minutes, until lightly toasted.

In a bowl, mix yogurt with 1 tsp. sugar and cinnamon; set aside. When pumpkin is soft, cut in half if necessary, remove and discard seeds, scoop out pumpkin flesh and coarsely mash flesh with a potato masher. Mix mashed pumpkin with sautéed apples and place in an ovenproof serving dish. Top with yogurt mixture and bake until heated through, about 5 minutes. Sprinkle with nuts and parsley and serve.

SPICY PUMPKIN BREAD

This is great when you are awash in Halloween pumpkin; or, you can use canned pumpkin. It makes a great holiday bread. It's just as easy to make 2 breads: keep one in the freezer or toast slices for a wonderful snack. To make pumpkin puree, bake a whole small pumpkin at 350° for about 50 minutes or more. Peel, remove seeds and puree pumpkin flesh with a food processor.

2 eggs
½ cup vegetable oil
½ cup milk or water
1 cup unsweetened pumpkin puree, fresh or canned
¾ cup sugar
2 cups all-purpose flour
1 tsp. baking soda
1 tsp. cinnamon
½ tsp. nutmeg
½ tsp. ground allspice
¼ tsp. ground cloves
½ tsp. salt
1 cup golden raisins
½ cup coarsely chopped walnuts

Heat oven to 350°. In a large bowl, whisk together eggs, oil and water. Add pumpkin and sugar and stir to combine. In another bowl, combine flour with baking soda, spices and salt. Add raisins and nuts to flour mixture and stir to coat. Pour flour mixture into egg mixture and mix just enough to combine. Transfer mixture to a greased 9-x-5-x-3-inch loaf pan and bake for about 1 hour or more, until a toothpick inserted in the center comes out clean. Cool on a wire rack.

BAKED ACORN SQUASH
WITH ORANGE GLAZE

This fall vegetable goes well with any roasted meat or, eaten cold, makes a quick and nutritious lunch. The glaze can be prepared in advance.

4 acorn squash, cut in half lengthwise
salt and pepper to taste
1 can (6 oz.) frozen orange juice
    concentrate, thawed
1 cup orange juice
about 2 tsp. freshly grated
    orange peel (zest)
½ cup brown sugar, packed
¼ cup butter
½ tsp. salt
½ tsp. nutmeg

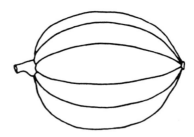

Heat oven to 425°. Remove seeds and membranes from squash and season with salt and pepper. Place squash cut-side down in a baking dish. Add about ½-inch water to dish, cover tightly with aluminum foil and bake for 40 to 45 minutes, until squash is almost tender.

In a medium saucepan, combine remaining ingredients. Bring to a boil, reduce heat to low and simmer uncovered for about 30 minutes, stirring occasionally, until syrupy.

Remove squash from oven and discard water. Turn squash cut side up and pour 2 tbs. of the orange glaze into each half. Reduce oven heat to 350°. Bake squash uncovered for about 20 minutes, basting occasionally with additional glaze, until squash is brown and very tender.

BAKED BUTTERNUT
SQUASH WITH APPLES

This is a superb addition to any poultry meal and is a special Thanksgiving treat. Butternut squash has a pear-like shape with a tan skin. Try to find squash with a long, thin upper portion. A short, squat squash will have many more seeds.

2 lb. or more butternut squash
1½ lb. or more Granny Smith apples, peeled, cored, quartered
½ cup dried currants
salt and pepper to taste
½ tsp. cinnamon
¼ tsp. nutmeg
½ cup pure maple syrup
¼ cup butter, melted
2 tbs. lemon juice

Heat oven to 350°. Pierce squash with a fork in many places. Place squash on a baking sheet and bake for about 10 minutes. Peel squash with a vegetable peeler and cut into slices about ½-inch thick. Combine squash pieces, apples and currants in a baking dish. Sprinkle with salt, pepper, cinnamon and nutmeg. Combine maple syrup, butter and lemon juice and pour over squash mixture. Toss to coat evenly. Bake for about 1 hour, stirring occasionally. Squash and apples should be very tender, but not mushy. This dish can be prepared ahead and reheated for about 15 minutes.

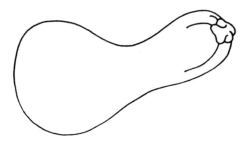

CURRIED SQUASH BISQUE

This is a lovely fall soup. The leeks must be thoroughly washed, unless you enjoy sand in your soup. The proportions can be varied to taste. You don't have to waste time chopping the vegetables into neat pieces; they all go in the food processor. If making ahead, place the shredded apple for garnish in lemon water to keep the apple from turning brown; drain before using.

¼ cup butter
1 bunch leeks, thoroughly washed, white part coarsely chopped
2-3 medium onions, coarsely chopped
2 tbs. curry powder, or to taste
1 large potato, peeled, chopped
3 lb. butternut squash or other winter squash, peeled, seeds and fibers removed, coarsely chopped

2 large Granny Smith or other tart baking apples, peeled, chopped
4 cups chicken stock
salt and pepper to taste
3 tbs. chopped fresh cilantro
1-2 tsp. grated fresh ginger
1 cup apple cider, or more if needed
shredded apple for garnish
chopped fresh cilantro for garnish

Melt butter in a large saucepan over medium heat. Add leeks, onions and curry powder. Cover pan and cook vegetables for about 10 minutes. Add potato, squash, apples, stock, salt, pepper, cilantro and ginger. Cover and cook for about 20 minutes, until vegetables are very soft. Puree mixture with a food processor until very smooth. Return mixture to saucepan, add cider if needed to reach desired consistency and heat through. Garnish with shredded apple and cilantro and serve.

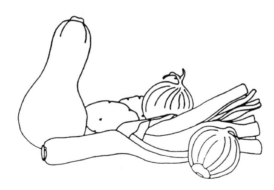

BAKED DELICATA SQUASH

Servings: 6

This sweet squash is so delicious that it needs very little adornment. Just bake it and top with melted butter and chopped parsley or dill.

2 delicata squash, about 2 lb.
1-2 tbs. butter
1 tbs. brown sugar, or to taste,
    optional
salt and pepper to taste
chopped fresh flat-leaf parsley or
    dill for garnish

Heat oven to 350°. Cut squash in half lengthwise and remove seeds and membranes. Place squash in a baking dish cut-side up. Add about 1/4 inch water to dish, cover dish with aluminum foil and bake for about 25 minutes, until squash is tender. About 5 minutes before squash is done, add butter, sugar, if using, salt and pepper and continue baking. Garnish with chopped parsley.

MUSHROOMS IN WINE

This recipe can be made with white mushrooms or a combination of domestic and wild varieties. Portobellos or shiitakes make this dish special. Mushrooms should never be soaked; wash them quickly, if necessary.

1/4 cup butter
1 cup minced onion
1 1/2 lb. mushrooms, sliced
2 tbs. flour
1/3 cup water
1/4 cup dry sherry or Madeira wine
1/2 cup sour cream or plain yogurt
1/4 cup chopped fresh flat-leaf parsley or
   dill, plus more for garnish
salt and pepper to taste
chopped fresh flat-leaf parsley for garnish

In a large skillet, melt butter over medium heat. Add onion and sauté until golden. Add mushrooms and sauté for about 5 minutes, stirring occasionally. Combine flour and water and add to mushrooms with sherry. Cook gently, stirring until smooth and slightly thickened. Add sour cream, parsley, salt and pepper and heat through; do not boil. Garnish with additional parsley. Serve immediately.

MUSHROOMS AND
ONIONS IN SOUR CREAM

Yogurt can be substituted for all or part of the sour cream without spoiling this dish. A combination of several kinds of mushrooms is an elegant touch.

1/4 cup butter
2 onions, thinly sliced
1 1/2 lb. mixed fresh mushrooms
1 cup sour cream or plain yogurt
1 tbs. lemon juice
salt and pepper to taste
1 tbs. chopped fresh flat-leaf parsley

In a heavy skillet, melt butter over medium heat. Add onions and cook until limp, about 3 to 4 minutes. Add mushrooms and cook over medium-high heat for 3 to 4 minutes. Reduce heat to low, add sour cream, lemon juice, salt and pepper and stir until cream is heated through; do not boil or cream will curdle. Add chopped parsley and serve.

WILD MUSHROOM HASH

This recipe is very different from what most people think of as hash. It makes a great side dish or a lunch. Use at least 3 different varieties of mushrooms, if possible, such as a combination of morel, portobello, shiitake and white mushrooms.

1/4 cup butter
1 1/2 lb. mixed mushrooms
2 cloves garlic, finely minced
1 red or green bell pepper, chopped
3-4 green onions, chopped
2 large potatoes, cooked, cubed
2 tbs. chopped fresh dill
salt and pepper to taste
dash cayenne pepper

Melt butter in a large skillet over medium-high heat. Add mushrooms, garlic, pepper and green onions and sauté until just tender, about 5 minutes. Add cooked potato, dill, salt, pepper and cayenne. Cook, stirring gently, until well combined. Serve immediately.

SWISS CHARD AND RICE

Swiss chard, like spinach, shrinks as it cooks. Although 2 bunches sound like a lot, you have to allow for shrinkage.

2 bunches Swiss chard, about 2 lb.
1 tbs. olive oil
1 cup chopped onion
3 cloves garlic, minced
1 large red bell pepper, coarsely
    chopped

2 cups cooked long-grain rice
1 tbs. soy sauce, or more to taste
1/4 tsp. nutmeg
dash cayenne pepper
1/2 cup grated sharp cheddar cheese

Wash chard thoroughly, but do not dry. Remove coarse stems from Swiss chard and dice. Remove tender stems and chop coarsely. Cut leaves crosswise into 1/2-inch strips. Heat olive oil in a large skillet. Add coarse chard stems, onion, garlic and red pepper and cook over medium-high heat, stirring occasionally, until onion is translucent and pepper is tender, about 3 minutes. Add tender chard stems and chard leaves and cook until leaves are limp, about 3 minutes. Add rice, soy sauce, nutmeg and red pepper and cook until heated through. Place vegetables in a serving dish and sprinkle cheese over the top.

SWISS CHARD BRAISED WITH CILANTRO

Servings: 6

Swiss chard is a leafy vegetable like kale and spinach. The stems can be tough, so they should be trimmed and diced before combining with the leaves.

3 large bunches Swiss chard, about 3 lb.
3-4 green onions, finely sliced
2 cloves garlic, minced
1/2 cup chopped fresh cilantro
1/3 cup olive oil
juice of 1/2 lemon, or more to taste
1 tsp. paprika
salt and pepper to taste
1/4 cup water

Wash chard thoroughly, but do not dry. Remove coarse stems from Swiss chard and dice. Remove tender stems and chop coarsely. Cut leaves crosswise into 1-inch strips. Place all ingredients in a heavy wide saucepan. Cover and cook over low heat for about 45 minutes, stirring occasionally to prevent sticking. Correct seasonings before serving.

BLACK-EYED PEAS
AND MUSTARD GREENS

Servings: 6-8

This hearty combination makes a tasty vegetarian meal or side dish for fish or meat. You can add other fresh herbs or substitute collard greens or kale for mustard greens.

2 cups dried black-eyed peas, rinsed
3-4 cloves garlic, or less to taste, cut into pieces
2 tbs. olive oil
2-4 tbs. minced garlic
1 lb. mustard greens, tough stems removed, thoroughly
    washed, coarsely chopped
2 tbs. chopped fresh thyme, oregano or basil, or 1 tsp. dried
salt and pepper to taste
2 cups cooked long-grain rice
2 tbs. lemon juice
chopped green or red onion for garnish
lemon wedges for garnish

Place black-eyed peas and garlic pieces in a large heavy saucepan with water to cover. Bring to a boil, reduce heat to low and cook for about 1 hour, stirring occasionally and adding more water if necessary, until peas are tender. If water has not been absorbed when peas are tender, drain. Set cooked peas aside in a large bowl.

Heat olive oil in a large skillet over medium heat. Add minced garlic and sauté for a few minutes, until limp. Add greens, with water still clinging to them, and herbs and stir-fry until greens are just wilted, no more than 5 minutes. Add cooked greens to cooked black-eyed peas and mix. Serve over cooked rice that has been mixed with lemon juice. Garnish with chopped onion and lemon wedges.

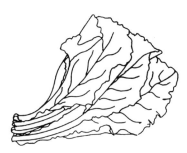

PECAN-VEGETABLE RICE

This vegetable-rice combination goes with pork or poultry or is a vegetarian entrée all by itself. The variety of textures and colors makes this a special addition to a holiday table.

2 cups chicken stock
1 cup long-grain rice
3 tbs. butter
½ cup pecan halves
4 green onions, chopped
1 clove garlic, minced
½ lb. white mushrooms, sliced
½ red bell pepper
½ yellow bell pepper
1 cup frozen petite peas, thawed
2 tbs. dry sherry
1 tbs. frozen orange juice concentrate, thawed
salt and pepper to taste

In a saucepan, bring chicken stock to a boil. Stir in rice and return to a boil. Reduce heat to low, cover and simmer for 20 minutes.

Melt butter in a skillet over medium heat. Add pecans and toss for about 2 minutes. Add green onions, garlic, mushrooms and bell peppers and sauté for about 3 to 5 minutes. Add peas and cook for 1 minute. Add sherry, orange juice concentrate, salt and pepper. Toss to heat through and mix with rice. Serve immediately.

LENTIL SOUP WITH ANCHO CHILE PASTE

A hearty chile paste is the perfect addition to lentil soup. This full-flavored dish can be a meal — just add a loaf of bread and a salad.

½ lb. green lentils
4 dried ancho chiles
1 cup hot water
½ tsp. ground allspice
⅛ tsp. ground cloves
3 tsp. ground cumin
½ tsp. dried rosemary
salt and pepper to taste
1-2 tbs. tomato paste
1 medium onion, minced
2 cloves garlic, minced
1 tbs. olive oil
8 cups water
2 tsp. grated fresh orange peel (zest)
1 bay leaf
1 cup sour cream or yogurt
¼ cup minced fresh cilantro, or more to taste

Heat oven to 200°. Sort lentils and wash once or twice; drain and set aside. Place chiles on a baking sheet and bake for 5 to 6 minutes, until limp. Remove and discard chile seeds and stems. Place chiles in a bowl and cover with 1 cup hot water. Cover bowl and let stand for about 5 minutes. Remove chiles from soaking liquid, reserving liquid, and combine chiles with spices and tomato paste in a food processor workbowl or blender container. Process mixture until smooth.

In a large saucepan, sauté onion and garlic in olive oil over medium heat until soft, about 5 minutes. Add chile mixture and sauté for a few minutes, stirring constantly. Add washed lentils, 8 cups water, reserved chile-soaking liquid, orange peel and bay leaf. Bring to a boil, reduce heat to low, partially cover and simmer slowly for about 1 hour, or until lentils are soft. Stir occasionally.

Remove soup from heat and cool slightly. Stir in sour cream; do not boil after sour cream is added, as it will curdle. Correct seasonings, sprinkle with cilantro and serve.

CHUNKY VEGETARIAN CHILI

Add a salad to this and you've got a healthy, satisfying meal. If you prefer a non-vegetarian meal, sauté ½ lb. lean ground beef with the peppers and onion.

1 tbs. olive oil
1 medium-sized green bell pepper, chopped
1 medium-sized red bell pepper, chopped
1 medium onion, chopped
3 cloves garlic, minced
2 cans (15 oz. each) Mexican-style tomatoes with juice
1 can (15 oz.) red kidney beans, rinsed, drained
1 can (15 oz.) pinto beans, rinsed, drained
1 can (15 oz.) whole-kernel corn, drained
1 cup long-grain rice
2½ cups water
salt and pepper to taste
2 tbs. chili powder
1 tsp. ground cumin, or more to taste
plain yogurt or sour cream for garnish, optional
chopped fresh cilantro for garnish, optional

In a 3-quart saucepan, heat olive oil over medium-high heat. Sauté peppers, onion and garlic until tender, about 5 minutes. Add remaining ingredients, except garnishes, and bring to a boil. Cover, reduce heat to low and simmer for about 30 minutes, stirring occasionally, until rice is tender. Serve immediately topped with yogurt and chopped cilantro if desired.

YEAR-ROUND VEGETABLE DISHES

SHALLOT VINAIGRETTE

The addition of shallots to this simple vinaigrette takes it out of the ordinary. The vinaigrette can keep, covered, in the refrigerator for up to 1 week. It makes a zingy salad dressing and can be used to top cauliflower, green beans or other vegetables.

½ cup coarsely chopped shallots
⅓ cup white wine vinegar
2-3 tbs. balsamic vinegar
1 tsp. Dijon mustard, or more to taste
1 tbs. chopped fresh tarragon, or 1 tsp. dried, optional
salt and pepper to taste
¾ cup extra virgin olive oil

Process all ingredients, except oil, with a mixer or food processor until smooth. With the machine running, slowly add oil and process until oil is incorporated and ingredients are well mixed.

CRISPY FRIED ONION AND APPLE FRITTERS

This is a wonderful "go-with" for roasted pork or chicken. The edges of the fritters should be browned; the rest of the fritter should be slightly crunchy. A food processor makes quick work of the chopping.

⅓ cup cornmeal
½ cup flour, or more if needed
2 tsp. sugar, or less to taste
2 tsp. baking powder
salt and pepper to taste
¾ cup milk
2 tbs. butter, melted
2 cups chopped yellow onions
1 cup peeled chopped apple
2 tbs. snipped fresh chives
vegetable oil for frying

In a large bowl, combine all ingredients, except vegetable oil, to form a batter. Add more flour if batter seems too runny.

Heat oven to 200°. In a large skillet, heat about ¼-inch oil until very hot. Drop heaping tablespoonfuls of batter into hot oil, flattening slightly with the back of spoon. Cook until brown on both sides; drain on paper towels and keep warm in oven. Do not crowd fritters or stack them, or they will turn soggy. Serve immediately.

BRAISED CELERY

Celery served with cheese and breadcrumbs is anything but ordinary. Braising brings out the flavor of the celery. This dish goes with everything.

½ cup chicken stock
½ cup dry vermouth
2 tbs. lemon juice
1 tsp. fennel seeds
12 black peppercorns
½ tsp. salt
6 large celery hearts, halved crosswise, quartered lengthwise
⅓ cup grated Parmesan cheese
⅓ cup fresh breadcrumbs
2 tbs. butter

In a large skillet, combine stock, vermouth, lemon juice, fennel seeds, peppercorns and salt. Add celery hearts and bring to a boil. Cover, reduce heat to low and simmer until just tender when pierced with a knife, about 15 minutes. Heat oven to 350°. Remove celery from braising liquid and keep warm. Continue cooking braising liquid over medium heat until reduced to about 1/3 cup, about 15 to 20 minutes. Place celery in a buttered baking dish and pour reduced braising liquid over celery. Combine Parmesan cheese and breadcrumbs and sprinkle over celery. Dot with butter. Bake until golden brown, about 15 minutes. Serve hot.

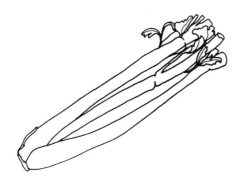

BAKED GARLIC BULBS

Servings: 6

Baked garlic makes an unusual appetizer spread on sliced French bread. Or, use it as an addition to mashed potatoes. When garlic is baked it loses its strong flavor and becomes mild and mellow. You can now purchase "garlic bakers," baking dishes that are specifically designed for baking garlic, at kitchenware stores.

6 whole firm bulbs garlic, outer paperlike skin
   removed, do not separate into cloves
1/4 cup olive oil
1/2 tsp. mixed dried Italian herbs, or more to taste
sliced French bread
olive oil for dipping, optional

Heat oven to 375° Place garlic in a small baking dish just large enough to hold bulbs upright. Brush bulbs with 1/4 cup olive oil and bake until garlic is soft when squeezed, about 40 to 45 minutes.

To serve, cut each bulb in half horizontally and squeeze garlic pulp from skins onto slices of French bread. For a special treat, dip bread slices into olive oil before squeezing garlic pulp onto them.

BROILED VEGETABLES WITH HERBS

Servings: 6-8

Use a combination of vegetables, such as carrots, Japanese eggplant, potatoes, turnips, zucchini or others. Slice them all about 1/4-inch thick.

about 3 lb. mixed sliced vegetables
3 tbs. lemon juice
vegetable oil
1-2 tsp. mixed dried basil, oregano and thyme
2-3 tbs. lime juice
chopped fresh basil, oregano and/or thyme for garnish, optional

Place vegetables and lemon juice in a large saucepan and cover with water. Cover and simmer over medium-low heat for about 15 minutes, until slightly underdone. Drain vegetables, pat dry and place on a large baking sheet. Heat broiler. Coat vegetables with oil and sprinkle with dried herbs. Broil vegetables for about 6 to 8 minutes, turning once. Place vegetables in a large serving dish and sprinkle with lime juice and fresh herbs, if using. Cover with aluminum foil until ready to serve.

24-HOUR LAYERED SALAD

This salad is best when made 24 hours ahead of time, but it should stand for at least 12 hours to blend the flavors. It is a great addition to any picnic. All ingredients should be free of excess moisture before layering.

2 bunches fresh spinach, about 1 lb., thoroughly
   washed and dried, stems removed
salt and pepper to taste
6 slices bacon, cooked, crumbled
3 hard-cooked eggs, sliced
1 pkg. (10 oz.) frozen peas, thawed
1 can (6 oz.) sliced water chestnuts, drained
1 purple onion, thinly sliced, or ½ cup thinly sliced green onions
½ cup thinly sliced radishes
1 cup sour cream, or a mixture of sour cream and plain yogurt
1 cup mayonnaise
6 oz. blue cheese, mashed
½ cup Spanish peanuts

Tear spinach leaves into small pieces and place in an 11-x-14-inch dish or wide-bottomed bowl. Season with salt and pepper and toss well. Layer with bacon, eggs, peas, water chestnuts, onion and radishes. Combine sour cream, mayonnaise and cheese and spoon over the top of salad, making sure the dressing covers the entire surface of salad. Cover tightly with plastic wrap and store in the refrigerator. Just before serving, top with peanuts.

COUNTRY-STYLE MIXED VEGETABLES

Servings: 6

This colorful dish can be prepared ahead and reheated, and it combines perfectly with broiled or grilled meat or fish.

2 tbs. olive oil
4 large yellow or Vidalia onions, coarsely chopped
3 cloves garlic, coarsely chopped
1 lb. yellow crookneck squash or zucchini,
  cut into matchstick strips or sliced
1/2 lb. portobello or other mushrooms, sliced
3 stalks celery, sliced
1 large red bell pepper, sliced
1 can (16 oz.) whole plum tomatoes, drained
1 cup dry white wine
1/4 cup minced fresh flat-leaf parsley
1/2 tsp. crushed dried tarragon, or more to taste

Heat olive oil over medium-high heat in a large skillet. Add onions, garlic, squash, mushrooms, celery and bell pepper and sauté, stirring often, until all vegetables are tender-crisp, about 10 minutes. Add tomatoes and wine and cook over high heat until most of the liquid is absorbed. Stir often to prevent burning. Add parsley and tarragon and heat through. Serve immediately or hold for later use.

MARINATED VEGETABLES

This can be prepared early in the day for a buffet item or salad. It is colorful and irresistible, so make a little more than you think you'll need.

2-3 cups broccoli florets
2-3 cups cauliflower florets
1/2 lb. fresh green beans, ends trimmed, cut into 2-inch pieces
2-3 cups baby carrots, whole or cut in half
2 cups small cherry tomatoes
1/2 cup chopped red onion or green onions
1/3 cup olive oil
1/4 cup red wine vinegar
1/4 cup Dijon mustard
1 tsp. sugar
1 tsp. mixed dried Italian herbs
salt and pepper to taste
1/3 cup coarsely chopped oil-packed sun-dried tomatoes
chopped fresh basil to taste, optional

Steam broccoli, cauliflower, beans and carrots until just tender-crisp, no more than 5 minutes. Rinse vegetables under cold running water, drain well and place in a large bowl with cherry tomatoes and onion. In a small bowl, whisk together olive oil, vinegar, mustard, sugar, herbs, salt and pepper. Pour mixture over vegetables, tossing to coat well. Chill for at least 2 hours, stirring occasionally. Add sun-dried tomatoes and stir. Just before serving add basil, if using.

VEGETABLES WITH LINGUINE

Servings: 6

This can be a vegetarian meal or filling side dish. You can add other vegetables, such as carrots or green beans. It's even good cold.

½ lb. dried linguine
½ cup ricotta or cottage cheese
⅓ cup grated Parmesan cheese or combination of Parmesan and Romano
½ head cauliflower, cut into florets
½ head broccoli, cut into florets
2 tbs. butter
2 tbs. olive oil
2 cloves garlic, minced
1 medium onion, chopped
½ lb. mushrooms, any type or combination, sliced
salt and pepper to taste
¼ tsp. red pepper flakes, optional
2 tbs. chopped fresh dill, or 1 tsp. dried
grated Parmesan cheese for garnish

Cook linguine in a large amount of boiling salted water until slightly firm to the bite, *al dente*. Drain and toss with a little olive oil to prevent sticking.

Combine ricotta and 1/3 cup Parmesan cheese; set aside. Steam cauliflower and broccoli florets until slightly undercooked, no more than 5 minutes; drain. In a large skillet, heat butter and olive oil over medium heat. Add garlic and onion and sauté until limp. Add mushrooms, salt, pepper, red pepper flakes, if using, and dill and sauté for 2 minutes. Stir in cauliflower and broccoli and continue cooking, stirring to combine ingredients. If mixture seems too dry, add a little water. Cook for about 5 minutes; do not overcook vegetables.

Pile linguine on a large serving plate. Spread cheese mixture over linguine and top with vegetable mixture. Garnish with additional grated Parmesan cheese and serve immediately.

VEGETABLE STROGANOFF

Servings: 6 or more

For this recipe, use 1, 2 or even 5 vegetables topped with a mushroom sauce. It's a good way to get rid of the small quantities of vegetables that often accumulate in the refrigerator.

¾ lb. dried egg noodles
5 tbs. butter
½ lb. chopped white, portobello or other mushrooms
1 cup chopped onion
salt and pepper to taste
2 tbs. chopped fresh dill, or 1 tsp. dried
2 tbs. chopped fresh tarragon, or 1 tsp. dried
1 tbs. soy sauce
¼ cup dry red wine
2 cups sour cream, plain yogurt or a combination
6-8 cups raw vegetables, such as baby carrots, broccoli florets, Brussels sprouts,
    cauliflower florets, green beans and/or zucchini pieces
¼ cup minced green onions
2 tbs. chopped fresh dill

Cook noodles in a large amount of boiling salted water until slightly firm to the bite, *al dente*; drain, return to cooking pan and add 2 tbs. of the butter. Stir until noodles are coated with butter.

Melt remaining 3 tbs. butter in a skillet over medium heat. Add mushrooms and onion and sauté for about 5 minutes, until soft. Add salt, pepper, dill, tarragon, soy sauce and wine and simmer for a few minutes to combine. Stir in sour cream and heat until warmed through; do not boil. Set aside and keep warm.

Cut vegetables coarsely; baby carrots should be left whole. Steam vegetables until just tender, about 5 to 7 minutes; do not overcook.

Spread noodles on a large platter. Top with steamed vegetables and sour cream sauce. Sprinkle with green onions and dill and serve immediately.

CONFETTI SPAGHETTI

This recipe can be expanded to feed an army (a small one). You can add or subtract vegetables or seasonings. It is a meal in itself or an all-in-one side dish.

1 lb. dried spaghetti or linguine
3 tbs. butter
3 tbs. olive oil
1 cup minced onion
3 large cloves garlic, minced
3 stalks broccoli, coarsely chopped
2 cups cauliflower florets
1/4 lb. mushrooms, wild preferred, sliced
1 red bell pepper, diced
2 cups fresh or frozen peas
salt and pepper to taste
2 tbs. chopped fresh basil, or 1 tsp. dried
1/4 cup finely chopped fresh flat-leaf parsley
2 tbs. soy sauce, optional
3/4 cup grated sharp cheddar cheese
3/4 cup grated Parmesan cheese

Cook pasta in a large amount of boiling salted water until slightly firm to the bite, *al dente*; drain and transfer to a large bowl.

Heat butter and oil in a large heavy skillet over medium heat until bubbly. Add onion and garlic and sauté until limp, about 2 to 3 minutes. Add broccoli, cauliflower, mushrooms, red pepper and peas and sauté until just tender, about 5 minutes. Remove skillet from heat and add salt, pepper, basil, parsley and soy sauce; mix well. Add vegetable mixture and cheeses to bowl with pasta; toss and serve immediately.

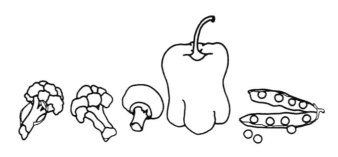

VEGETABLE-BULGUR PILAF

This recipe is quite versatile: you can add other vegetables; you can change the seasonings; you can omit the cheese; and you can use up leftovers that need eating. Bulgur wheat can be found in the supermarket near the rice, either in a box or in a bulk bin.

3 tbs. butter
2-3 zucchini, thinly sliced
1 cup sliced green onions
2 cloves garlic, minced
1 red bell pepper, coarsely chopped
2-3 carrots, diced
1½ cups bulgur wheat
2 cups chicken stock
1 tsp. mixed dried Italian herbs
salt and pepper to taste
1 can (1 lb.) stewed tomatoes, chopped
1 cup grated sharp cheddar cheese

Melt butter in a large skillet over medium-high heat. Add zucchini, green onions, garlic, pepper and carrots and sauté for 3 to 4 minutes, until vegetables are tender-crisp. Add bulgur and sauté for a few more minutes, until bulgur is coated with butter. Add stock, herbs, salt, pepper and tomatoes. Bring to a boil, cover, reduce heat to low and simmer until all liquid is absorbed, about 15 to 20 minutes. Spoon hot mixture into a serving dish and top with cheese. Let stand until cheese is slightly melted and serve immediately.

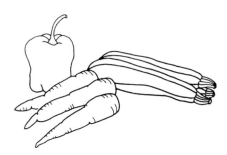

ROASTED VEGETABLES
WITH COUSCOUS

Servings: 6-8

This is an expandable recipe: you can add more vegetables if desired. If you don't want to use a packaged couscous mix, prepare couscous in your usual fashion and combine it with the roasted vegetables.

2 tbs. olive oil
3 medium onions, cut into wedges, or
  1 lb. small white onions, peeled
1 lb. zucchini, cut into 2-inch chunks
½ lb. baby carrots
10 cloves garlic, cut in half

1 tbs. mixed dried Italian herbs,
  or more to taste
1 tsp. sugar
salt and pepper to taste
1 can (28 oz.) whole tomatoes, drained
1 pkg. (10 oz.) instant couscous mix

Heat oven to 350°. Place olive oil, onions, zucchini, carrots, garlic, herbs, sugar, salt and pepper in a large bowl and toss well. Transfer to a large baking sheet and roast until vegetables are just tender-crisp, about 30 minutes. Add drained tomatoes, breaking large pieces with a fork. Keep vegetables warm. Make couscous according to package directions. Serve warm vegetables over couscous.

INDEX

SERVE CREATIVE, EASY, NUTRITIOUS MEALS WITH nitty gritty® cookbooks